AF602142

# My First Investment In Crypto and Stocks for Teens

---

*A Dummies' Guide to Investing in*

*Cryptocurrency and the Stock Market for Teenagers and Beginners*

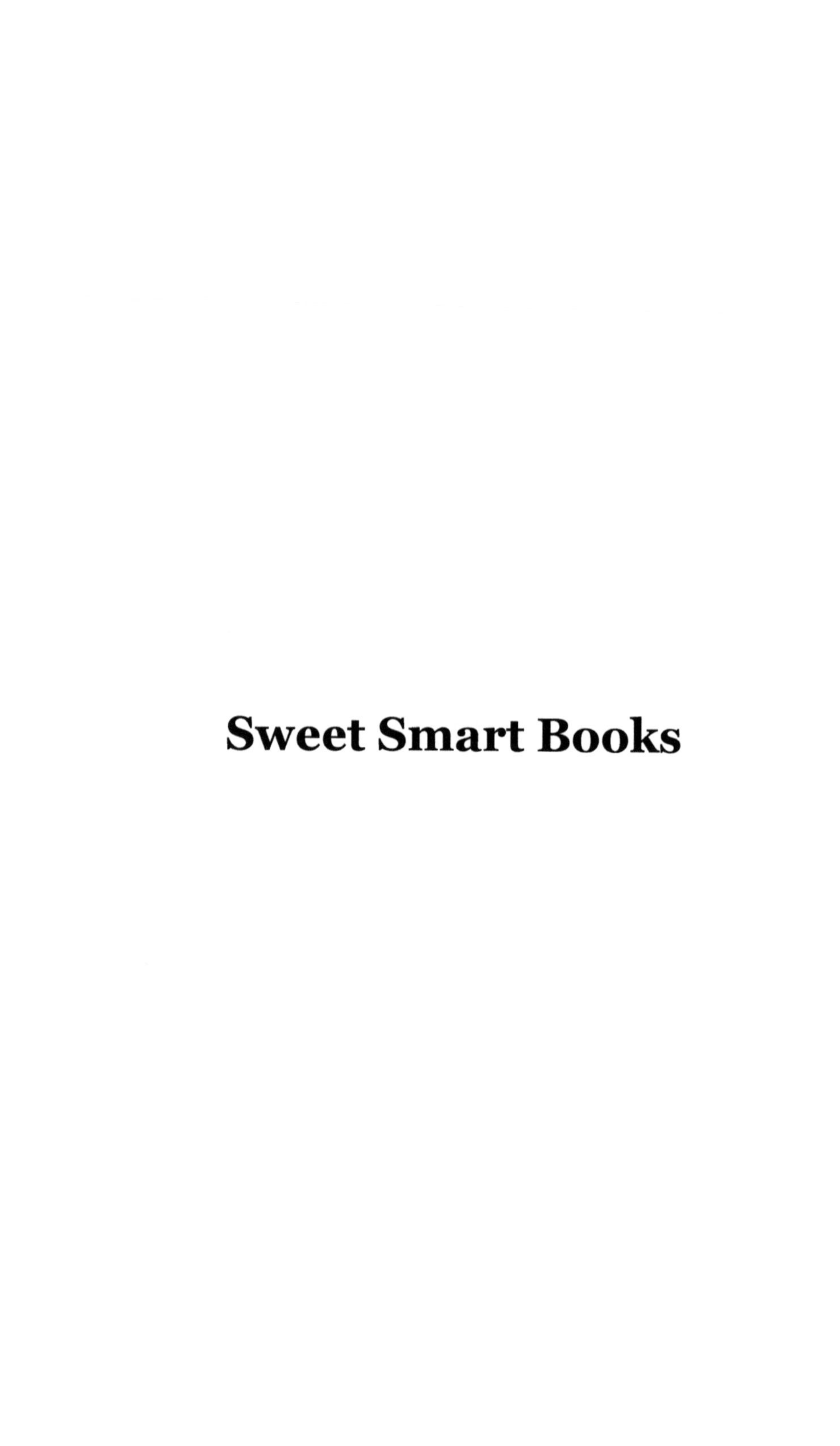

**Sweet Smart Books**

# Table of Content

# Introduction

Investing is always a great opportunity for individuals to achieve financial independence. We all know how important financial stability is to leading a better life. The global pandemic that struck the world in the form of Covid-19 just a year back has made people realize how important it is to have savings to deal with black swan events that come out of nowhere and cripple us. The financial world is now full of opportunities for beginners and experienced investors. The success of cryptocurrencies has widely helped people understand the difference between centralization and decentralization. On the other hand, events like "The Big Squeeze" have helped the financial world understand the importance of retail investors and their role in influencing the markets.

As a teen, you might have less knowledge about different markets, unlike a veteran who constantly looks at the market to make their financial decisions over a long period of time. It is common for teens to ignore the importance of investing from a young age. Less than 5% of teens will start reading about finance when they are just entering college. If you are reading this book, then I am sure that you fall under that 5% who are enthusiastic about gaining financial independence as soon as possible. As veteran traders, we will be helping you to understand different financial assets that can help you earn consistent returns in both short and long intervals. To be a great investor, you first need to be a great learner, for investors' knowledge is important.To that end, we will focus on providing you with the knowledge that can help you become skilled in different financial markets and assets.

## Why Is It Important to Invest Now?

Right now, the world is in a recovery stage and has been rebuilding its economy over the past few years following the onset of the global pandemic. The world is just leaving recession, and financial enthusiasts are expecting a bull market in all the global financial markets in the coming few years. Coming back from a recession is always a challenging task for local businesses and multinational companies. From the Great Depression to the housing bubble crisis, when fighting a recession, people and companies innovate more than usual, hence, there will be exponential growth leading to enormous returns for all investors.

With a small investment in the right company or cryptocurrency, you can achieve financial independence in the future. Investing promises you freedom and protects you from any other black swan events that may occur in the near future. Investing is the only weapon that you can hold in these uncertain times. Investing is not only a way to increase your wealth but also a backup security, especially during emergencies and uncertain situations.

## Why Should You Listen to Us?

Sweet Smart Books has helped thousands of investors to understand complex financial concepts readily. All our books have thoroughly researched up-to-date information that is explained in an easy and innovative way. We collect information curated by tens of financial authors to create a guide that can clear your confusion regarding financial assets and help you decide which financial asset is better for you according to your requirements and passion.

Before providing you with information about different financial markets and financial assets, we want you to review your goals for this journey. While it may be a fact that everyone needs money for survival, everything that investors can earn in these markets will be more valuable if they are genuinely excited about the investment that they are going to be a part of. If you are investing in Tesla, it is essential to be excited about their products and improvements in their automobile engineering technology. Your investment style will change with passion, and will result in a better overall return.

*A small checklist:*

Before starting investing in different financial assets, you must understand your current financial position as a beginner. As most of the readers reading this book are teens, we are providing a checklist for the teen demographic to help them easily assess their current financial position.

- Do you have any savings?
- Are they your savings or your parents'?
- Does your family carry any debts?
- How important is investing for you at this point?
- What is your immediate goal for investing?
- How much are you expecting to earn within five years by investing?
- Are you willing to work hard to research different financial assets?

## How Can This Book Help You?

Investing can indeed be overwhelming, especially for someone just starting in the world of finance. Some countless opportunities and strategies mentioned in this book can be used to double or triple your earnings within a short amount of time. However, not every method is reliable, and therefore, without a complete understanding of the basic building blocks of the investment world, you will start to crumble.

To get the most out of this book, we recommend you follow mind maps and learning techniques such as passive recall. We welcome you to the most exciting world of finance. We wish you all the best for your endeavor to learn more on this topic.

***Disclaimer:***

The author of this book has written it only to provide knowledge to the reader. All financial markets are volatile and hence, readers should not solely depend on this book to make financial decisions. The author of this book will in no way be responsible for the readers' financial decisions.

# Chapter 1: Introduction to Investing

Whether you are investing in Bitcoin, an IPO, a publicly traded company, or a real estate investment trust, everything can be called a financial asset. All these assets have the main motive of providing profits to the investor. Irrespective of whether you are a retail or institutional investor, it is essential to have a basic idea of what investing is and its history, in brief, to make your mark in the ever-expanding financial world.

This chapter is designed to help you focus on the bottom layer of the complex foundation block that needs to be mastered to succeed in the financial industry.

## History of Investing

Investing has existed right from the initial stages of civilization. While it is true that the value of different financial assets has changed over time, investment still exists and is probably the only way to achieve financial independence within very little time. As humans, we have always invested in one way or another.

Thousands of years ago, when humans were getting civilized, people used the barter system. It is a type of transaction system where humans can exchange items instead of currency to acquire what they need for survival. However, the barter system is not so perfect, and with time, as civilizations started to become overpopulated, people abolished it and started to use gold for all their transactions.

Gold is an evergreen way to exchange items. It existed for more than a thousand years as a transaction and investment value, but people started to observe the disadvantages associated with it over time. It isn't easy to carry gold or divide it whenever needed. As Gold is a free mineral and there were fewer restrictions back then, a few people became extremely rich, whereas others lived in poverty. Looking at the disadvantages associated with gold, banks started to distribute paper bills for all their account holders. With time, people began to trust this currency and soon, the modern world adopted fiat currency as a trusted transaction system. Even though we have different currencies worldwide now, it is a lot easier to make even foreign transactions with services such as Paypal and Payoneer.

From the 16th century, businesses started to bloom because of the initiation of the complex fiat currency system. Businesses such as the East Indian Company began to flourish in European countries. During these times, businesses needed a lot of capital to improve their businesses, and for the first time in modern financial history, the Amsterdam Stock Exchange was established to help companies gather initial investment from their citizens. Soon, stock markets started to pop up worldwide, marking the beginning of the modern financial era.

Stock markets flourished globally, and both businesses and the shareholders involved became rich. Banks started to approach this new situation by providing new financial assets such as fixed deposits and mutual funds to their customers. In the initial days, all these stock markets were barely regulated, making them vulnerable to future financial crises. Events like the Tulip Bulb crisis and The Great Depression have helped financial experts and ordinary people understand why governments should regulate investments. Over time, both congress and the Federal Reserve have created institutes such as the Security Exchanges Commission (SEC) to control different financial markets and approaches.

By the end of 2000, stock markets controlled the world economy, challenging even governments. With the internet, the opportunities have increased for retail investors and reduced the power of big players such as hedge funds, who are always considered ruthless monopolies in the financial markets. Events such as the Internet Bubble and Housing Bubble crisis have helped shape the modern financial markets and helped people realize the importance of decentralized financial assets. Bitcoin emerged into the financial world during these times, showing its impact within a few short years.

In 2021, during an ongoing pandemic that has crippled the world economy, investments were not only a choice for most individuals but were also essential. Desk jobs don't give you enough money or savings to lead a blessed life, and only investments with smart decisions and willpower can.

## Five Simple Rules of Investing

Investing is universal, and how to invest changes according to your conditions. Many beginners usually try to learn strategies that may not work out for them immediately because of insufficient investment capital, insufficient experience to understand the actual trends, or an inability to predict the black swan events that may occur in the future.

To help beginners understand the core foundations of investing, we have provided five basic rules that anyone, irrespective of their age or whereabouts, should follow in the financial world. Remember that investing is never complicated. It seems complex because of what we expect from these investments. Have a clear goal, and you will do fine along the road.

### 1. Be Early and Be Often

It is pretty hard to make people understand that investments can turn out better when you start earlier. Just take the example of a tree. When will it have grown more, when it was planted many times before? A young tree, however bright, cannot outgrow an already planted tree. Of course, sometimes there are exceptions. But for most of your investments to be fruitful, you need to be in the game as early as possible.

You also need to invest as often as possible, apart from being early. Make it a habit rather than looking at it as a burden. Having clear goals along with consistent investment can make your portfolio more diverse. Exponential growth can be possible only when you follow these two factors almost religiously. Don't worry about the amount you are investing; it will all add up in the future because of the wonders that compounding interest holds.

2. **Minimize Fees and Taxes**

To become successful with investing, you need to have the mindset to limit your fees and taxes as much as possible. As an investor, try to find brokers and resources that provide value for you with as little expense as possible. Make only one big trade per month instead of making a small trade every week.

Make the most out of the options that the government provides to minimize your taxes. Invest in mutual funds or insurance policies that offer IT returns for all citizens. Having a retirement account can also help you reduce some of your taxes for a better and more secure future after retirement.

3. **Diversification Is Important**

   It is essential not to invest all your money into just one asset as an investor. Never keep all your eggs in one basket because if something happens to that basket, then your financial status will be in jeopardy. This is the sole reason we have discussed many different financial assets in both the stock market and the blockchain ecosystem. Diversification also helps you experiment with new financial assets that can sometimes provide many returns.

4. **Do What Is Right for You**

   Every investor always has their own set of goals. Make clear goals according to your current life commitments and financial status. Focus on the financial assets that will take you nearer to your goal. If your goal is to have a safe retirement, start investing in assets that will appreciate over time. If you want to make some short, quick gains, begin trading or investing in volatile assets such as cryptocurrencies.

5. **Long-Term Goals Are More Important**

   Most of the investors' main goal is to secure their future and fulfill their long-term goals. While short-term earnings are wonderful, they can be easily lost if you don't have a solid portfolio and well researched risk-management strategies to secure these funds. As an investor, you should make every trade focused on your long-term goals. If an investment asset deviates from your future financial goals in any way, then it may not be a great investment idea. List your long-term goals and create a new pathway for your financial independence.

## Different Types of Investing

Investment can be of many types. As an individual, you first need to make sure which tactic you are comfortable with before learning about different financial assets. Each tactic has its advantages and disadvantages.

1. **Active Investing**

   Active investing is an investment strategy where the investor will be actively involved in daily trades. For an active investor, investment is their sole job and purpose. Most retail intraday traders, mutual fund managers, and hedge fund employees fall under this category. Active investing is challenging and requires a lot of knowledge, networking, and patience.

2. **Passive Investing**

   Passive investing is an investment strategy where individuals depend on other expert decisions or rely on the market movements. Even though passive investors dedicate less time to fundamental analysis, they aim for potential long-term growth. Passive investing is considered risk-free and promises better returns when compared to other investment strategies.

3. **Growth Investing**

   Growth investing is an investment strategy where individuals will dedicate most of their portfolio to investing in assets that show substantial potential growth in the next few years. Stocks such as Tesla and cryptocurrencies such as Ethereum are great examples of assets for growth investing. Growth investors often depend on extraordinary jumps in profits to judge whether or not a financial asset is the best investment choice.

4. **Value Investing**

   Value investing is an investment strategy where individuals will dedicate most of their portfolios to investing in financial assets that are already proven worthy. Value investing is risk-free, but the returns are minimal compared to assets that belong to the growth sector. Dividend investing can be a great example of value investing.

Before going on to learn about different financial investment strategies in much more detail, you first need to have a good overview of the various available financial assets.

## Different Financial Assets

Financial assets are intangible, and their ownership can be easily exchanged for fiat money. When you buy a financial asset, you acquire control to hold the asset's value. Some financial assets provide you with little returns, such as in the form of dividends or interests. The modern financial world is heavily dependent on these financial assets to stabilize the economy.

All the financial assets can be easily converted into cash, and the ownership of all these assets can usually be proven using certificates and legal documents. If you want to get hold of a financial asset, you need to meet a seller willing to sell these assets for you in return for cash. You can do the same if you want to sell your current financial assets. The internet and institutions like the SEC have made these transactions easy, sometimes just with a mouse click. While many financial assets can provide you with high value, this book focuses more on stocks and cryptocurrencies for the reader.

- **Cash Deposits**

  The most common way to earn savings is by accruing interest for the money saved in your bank accounts. A unique form of a cash deposit that is locked down for a guaranteed profit is known as a fixed deposit. However, you cannot withdraw your money into your bank account before the lockdown date without paying a penalty fee. Cash deposits are considered riskless investments but can provide fewer returns when compared to other financial assets that are out there.

- **Gold**

  Gold is a classic investment choice for many individuals and families in developing and underdeveloped countries. Gold value not only increases with time but can also help you to get easy personal loans with very little interest from banks and private entities.

- **Stocks**

  Stocks are financial assets that provide you with ownership for a part of a publicly traded company. Stocks are versatile financial assets that are easy to get into and are more popular with retail investors. Stocks also have excellent return value over time. You can invest in stocks with less research based on your long-term return expectations. However, earning short-term money with stocks is complicated and requires you to have sufficient knowledge about technical analysis as a prerequisite. Many stocks also provide dividends for all their shareholders.

- **Mutual Funds and ETFs**

  Both of these financial assets help you invest in many stocks at one time in different forms. A mutual fund allows you to place your money into a pool of funds where other investors are involved. On the other hand, an ETF helps you trade a group of stocks at once. Mutual funds and ETFs provide dividends for the investors, making them the most popular way to invest in stock markets with manageable risk and assured returns.

- **Derivatives**

  Derivatives are financial contracts that increase or decrease their value depending on the change in the underlying asset's value. Options contracts and futures contracts are some of the popular derivatives that are used in different financial markets. As an investor, you can use derivatives to secure your current portfolio or to earn steady passive income by writing derivative contracts.

- **Real Estate and REITs**

  Real estate is probably the most complex financial strategy to earn huge returns. It involves a lot of reconnaissance and networking to find exciting real estate projects that can provide huge returns over time. If you are not skilled enough to do all this, you can invest in REITs to invest in some of your favorite real estate properties without all the hard work.

- **Cryptocurrencies**

  Cryptocurrencies are the 21st-century digital currencies that shook the world by solving the problem of double-spending. All cryptocurrencies depend on blockchain technology to save all the transactions without users in the network being worried about the legitimacy of these transactions. Bitcoin, Ethereum and Ripple are considered life-changing financial assets due to their vast returns. Cryptocurrencies are also, however, considered volatile by most financial experts.

Apart from these financial assets, bonds, currency pairs, and investing in private businesses via crowdfunding are also rising in popularity with the young generation. Irrespective of the financial asset you choose to invest in, you need to research and calculate your estimated returns over time thoroughly. Remember that none of these financial assets provide guaranteed returns. You need to master skills that can help you find financial assets that will work for you over time. The following chapters of this book are solely designed to help you increase financial literacy to achieve skills that can pave a path to your financial independence.

# Chapter 2: Introduction to the Stock Market

Stock market investing is probably the most popular way to invest for beginners. Stock markets influence the world economy and can often determine the path of a country's economy. Stocks also provide decent returns for most investors, especially over the long term. To make the best returns from the stock market, you need to understand the bigger picture and analyze different players present in the market.

Remember that investing in stock markets is extremely risky. As veteran traders, we suggest you understand the basics mentioned in this chapter and crosscheck with your research before making a trading decision.

## What Are Stocks?

Stocks are financial assets that provide you with ownership for a part of a publicly traded company. Google, Tesla, and Microsoft are popular publicly traded companies in the U.S. stock market. You, as an investor, along with thousands of other investors, try to buy a fraction of the company in return hoping that its value will increase over some time. Companies use the money provided to them by holding stocks to develop infrastructure and services that are the foundation of their business.

The value of your stocks can increase over time if the company performs well, or can decrease in value if the company doesn't perform according to your expectations. As a stockholder, you will get the special privileges of reviewing the new company policies or during the appointment of the CEO. However, your powers are often neglected because many stockholders are holding the stock, and your sole decision will not be considered primary. However, collectively, stockholders can try to change the company's decisions.

In the 21st century, retail investors are essential for the growth of any public traded company. All the stock exchanges between two parties are usually handled by the exchange, such as the New York Stock Exchange (NYSE), which regulates when and how these transactions should happen.

# How Does the Stock Market Work?

Stocks are just certificates of part ownership of a company. When you buy a stock, a digital certificate will be generated for you on the exchange website where you bought those stocks. All stock transfers happen through a complex procedure involving many players. The stock lifecycle mentioned below will help you understand the complexity of stock markets from a big-picture perspective.

**Example:**

Sam, a rookie investor, decides to buy 100 shares of Microsoft with his savings. To convert his fiat money into certified stocks, Sam needs to be a part of the process that is mentioned below.

1. **Create a Brokerage Account**

   To make a stock transaction, Sam should first create a brokerage account. There are many stock brokerages available for investors on the internet. Robinhood is one of the popular stock brokerages for U.S. investors right now. Every country has their own approved stock brokerages, and it is therefore challenging to trade in different stock markets with just one stock brokerage. So, make sure that you know your country's regulations regarding brokerages before investing in them.

Make sure that they are legit by visiting the official SEC website to crosscheck their authenticity. Once you are sure, you can create a brokerage account by confirming your identity using the KYC compliance that all these brokerage institutes follow. Once your account is confirmed, open your account to deposit money and invest in different stocks.

2. **Order a Stock Transaction**

Now, open your brokerage account to look at the different available stocks for you to invest in. Click on the stock information and enter the number of stocks you are ready to buy from other investors. Once you confirm the order, your stock details will be sent to the exchange, such as the NYSE, to route it to another brokerage firm where investors are trying to sell their stocks. Once both of your requests are linked, the amount will be debited from the account, and the stocks will be immediately credited to your brokerage account.

Here, the SEC acts as a mediator to verify the authenticity of all the transactions happening. There is no chance of foul play being involved in any brokerages or the exchange itself. All the stock transactions will be performed only during the trading hours, and any transactions placed after the market trading hours will be cleared as soon as the market resumes the next day.

3. **Wait for the Value to Grow**

   Once the stocks are confirmed, you will become the rightful owner of these securities. Now, when they are in your possession, you can either lend them to other investors or just save them in your portfolio to earn passive income by writing call and put option contracts.

## Characteristics of Stocks

All stocks have some essential characteristics that have made them the most important financial assets in the real world.

1. **Stocks Are Non-refundable**

   All stocks have a value, and if you are not satisfied with the performance of a particular stock, your money will not be refunded. You can only sell it to other investors who are willing to buy it from you. This is the main reason why liquidity is significant for stocks.

2. **Stocks Give You Rights**

   Stocks provide you with investment value and will provide you with the right to participate in different company meetings and give you the ability to become a part of the company decision process.

3. **Stocks Provide You With Dividends**

   Just like interests that banks and other government institutes give you to store your money with them, some stocks provide you with consistent income known as dividends.

4. **Stocks Provide You With Derivatives**

   All stocks can be betted upon using derivatives such as options and futures to trade them. Many investors use the characteristic to protect their portfolio or earn additional income while holding the stocks.

5. **Stocks Cannot Expire**

   Stocks don't have an expiration date, and hence, they will not expire unless you want to sell them to other investors.

# Different Types of Stocks

Stocks are of different types and can vary according to different conditions. To better organize your portfolio, it is better to divide and organize stocks based on their performance.

Stocks can be of four types when divided based on the performance metrics.

1. **Growth Stocks**

   These are the stocks that have the potential for massive growth. Most of the growth stocks will be pretty new in the industry and challenge their competitors with their latest innovations. As growth stocks need to use all the capital to develop their services quickly, they will not give the investors any dividends. Tesla is an excellent example of a growth stock.

2. **Income Stocks**

   These are the already popular stocks due to their consistent growth over a long period. All these stocks provide a reasonable dividend yield ratio for all the stockholders. Apple and Microsoft are great examples of income stocks.

3. **Cyclic Stocks**

   These stocks are sensitive to market changes and black swan events but can provide huge returns when they are performing well. Technology stocks fall under this category.

4. **Non-Cyclic Stocks**

   These stocks don't depend on any other factors, such as market changes or market sentiment. Pharma stocks are an example of non-cyclic stocks in the market.

Stocks can also be divided into two types based on their legal obligations.

1. **Common Stocks**

   These are stocks where all the stockholders have the same value and rights, and all the stockholders will receive the same dividends.

2. **Preferred Stocks**

   These are stocks where few entities hold more power than the stockholders present. The preferred stockholders receive more dividends and are entitled to more rights than the regular stockholders.

## Fundamental Analysis

Fundamental analysis is a pioneer investment skill that investors have used to determine best-performing assets and invest in them for the past few decades. Fundamental analysts focus more on the long-term opportunities that these assets provide instead of on the short-term returns. As an investor, everyone needs to create their own fundamental analysis strategy according to their investment choices.

## *What Is Fundamental Analysis?*

Fundamental analysis helps investors decide when to buy a stock to have better profits. The primary goal of the fundamental analysis is to find whether or not the investment asset's intrinsic value will grow in the future. Finding the intrinsic value and the factors that affect this value is the most significant part of this process.

Investors need to use two major types of fundamental analysis tactics to get the accurate intrinsic value of different assets.

### Quantitative Analysis

The quantitative analysis describes the fundamental analysis technique where an investor mainly uses numbers to determine a financial asset's intrinsic value. Learning about some of the quantitative analysis factors can help you effectively understand the future movement of the asset value.

- **Balance Sheet**

  Balance sheets help you understand the overall value of a stock, company, or cryptocurrency you are investing in. By analyzing the balance sheet, you can guess whether a company is in profits or on the verge of losses. Balance sheets also help investors know the equity value of an asset or a company.

- **Income Statement**

  On the other hand, an income statement provides the profits or the revenue a publicly traded company has generated over a quarterly or a year. With a balance sheet, you can only judge the asset's market value, whereas an income statement can help you understand the market direction of the asset.

### Qualitative Analysis

Qualitative analysis is used to judge various factors that are not related to numbers and can affect the intrinsic value of a financial asset.

- **Business Model**

  An investor can decide whether or not a stock can perform well in the future by understanding the company's business model. Companies with rapid growth don't always have to display consistent growth. Understanding how the company is trying to price their services can help a fundamental analyst understand how they spend their capital investments.

- **Competitors**

  To understand a company's prospects, you need to study details about the company and its competitors. Companies fall short because they are defeated by their competitors most of the time. For example, the mobile phone pioneer in the early 2000s, Nokia, lost most of its market share because of not catching up with other smartphone companies' advancements. Understanding business models and linking them with other competitors' business models can also help you predict who will perform well in the future.

- **Management**

  Executives run companies, and their public image and decisions can affect their performance. Analyze different vital people who are managing the company and analyze their portfolio to understand their work culture. Satisfied employees can also help a company thrive in the long term.

To help investors perform fundamental analysis research more tactically, we have divided the most prevalent factors into three categories.

### *Macroeconomic Factors*

A country's growing economy and the economic policies being introduced will have a significant impact on the future of publicly traded companies. Both the stock market and economy are linked to each other in many ways, making the market react to even a negligible financial decision made by the government in the form of price change.

A fundamental analyst can predict these economic changes that can increase the intrinsic value of an asset over time. Here are some factors that you need to be aware of as an investor regarding macroeconomic factors.

**Impact of GDP**

A GDP is the most critical metric used to calculate its exchanges of imports based on all the businesses present. When a country is sending considerable imports to other countries, then the citizens' opportunities increase, leading to new businesses and overall economic growth. Countries with high GDP perform better in quarterly reports, making it a viable factor for investors to consider the economy's overall growth.

GDP reports are made public by the government every quarter. You can also use private agencies to be thorough with the data before they go public to predict the price changes of different assets before everyone else.

**Inflation**

Inflation is an economic concept where the price of products will change according to the supply and demand ratio present. Hyperinflation is caused when the country's production in different sectors decreases, increasing prices. Both an increase or decrease in the inflation rate can make businesses suffer in a country. As a fundamental analyst, you need to analyze how inflation is performing in a different sector to judge the intrinsic value of different companies in that sector.

### Interest Rates

Interest rates determine how a country's financial institutions and governments are performing. As is often the case, fewer interest rates increase the capital flow to businesses.

To calculate the interest rate, use the formula below:

Interest rate = Interest/principal

### Economic Cycle

Before investing in a stock, you also should consider the economic cycle and how it can affect the performance of your stock. An economic cycle usually consists of four stages.

1. **Prosperity**

   This is the initial stage where development and growth stay constant, helping new businesses to thrive. Investing in this stage provides huge immediate returns for the investors.

2. **Recession**

   This is the stage where the economic conditions will start to deteriorate majorly due to one or two mismanaged sectors. For example, the housing bubble crisis, which pushed the whole world into recessions, was caused by the fall of the U.S. real estate market. During a recession, people will lose jobs and the economy worsens, making businesses and investors lose wealth.

3. **Depression**

   After a recession, depression follows. This is an economic stage where bears will rule the market, leading to severe unemployment, unrest, and economic disruption. During the depression, it is not advised to invest in any financial asset opposite to the market sentiments. During this stage, you need to be aware of government policies and stimulus packages to revive the economy.

4. **Recovery**

   No one likes to stay calm when the world is in ruins. People will find ways to innovate and improve the economy. The young generation become saviors, and the economy will boom in this stage. The recovery phase is excellent for investors because many publicly traded companies are trying to become better with their services. A fundamental analyst usually searches for this phase while investing in stocks for the long term.

### Political Factors

In one way or another, all the financial markets can be influenced by the political factors that occur in the country. You need to closely follow these conditions and different monetary policies being implemented by the current government to estimate the market movement.

**Natural Factors**

While entirely beyond our ability to stop them, natural factors can also hurt the performance of various stocks. Earthquakes, tsunamis and global pandemics can cripple the world economy, leading to business decline. As a fundamental analyst, you cannot estimate these black swan events. Still, you should consider the possibility and create an exit strategy to not lose too much of your money during uncertain situations like this. An intelligent investor will always have an exit plan.

### *Industry Information*

With a good understanding of macroeconomic factors, you are set to continue your research with the industry metrics that influence the stock's performance.

To understand the market sentiment, you need first to classify different industries based on market capitalization, performance, and impact on the world economy. Industries can be divided into sub-sectors for better analysis and understanding of the market conditions.

What should you do?

- **Know What the Market Wants**

  Industry analysis should always focus on knowing what the people are rooting for. You can't invest in a gramophone company when people root for Ipods. Your fundamental analysis should understand consumer trends and reflect them in your choice of companies that can perform well in the future.

- **Understand Rules and Regulations**

  Each industry has its specifications to understand how a company is performing. You must understand the technical jargon involved with different industries and sub-sectors as an investor.

- **Understand the Basic Philosophy**

  To become better at fundamental analysis, imagine yourself as the consumer of the industry and the basic philosophy that got you hooked with the industry. For example, suppose you are investing in companies that create console games. In that case, you have to understand the philosophy surrounding console games and understand which companies are more ambitious and enthusiastic to create great products. Doing so can help you to understand your industry from the bigger picture.

## *Company Information*

Once the company analysis is done, you need to research the company itself. Not all information about companies will be publicly available for investors. You need to use premium services to get access to information that can help you judge whether a company is performing well according to the market expectations.

### Net Assets

Calculate the total net assets for the company and understand the number of debts that the company is currently at.

Net assets = Total assets - liabilities

### Use Reports

Analyze the earnings reports to check whether the company executives are hiding any information from the public. Many companies do this to cover their losses or manipulate investors to provide them with more capital.

### Analyze Management

As an investor, you also need to focus on the management controlling and utilizing the capital provided by the investors.

### Growth Percentage

Check the past year records and confirm whether the company's growth is increasing or declining. A company's performance is directly proportional to the number of investors joining to invest in a company.

What should you do next?

Once all the fundamental analysis factors are analyzed, you need to select stocks for your investment. Never invest all your capital into a single company, even if it satisfies all the conditions you are looking out for. Spread out and wait for the market to decide your fate. Use recommended risk-management strategies for your portfolio to save your capital. Even one terrible event can decrease the value of your holdings.

## Technical Analysis

While fundamental analysis entirely depends on research and reports to determine the price evaluation of a financial asset, technical analysis depends on supply and demand to determine the price movements of a financial asset. Day traders rigorously use technical analysis, trend traders, swing traders, and scalpers to make their trading decisions. While it is easy to start with technical analysis indicators using the resources available on the internet, you need a lot of determination to become proficient in the subject.

## *What Is Technical Analysis?*

Technical analysis is a financial investment philosophy where followers believe it is possible to determine the future prices of stocks based on the logical and statistical data already available on the market. By analyzing these historical trends, investors decide when to enter and exit a trade to increase their profits over time. However, technical analysis is proven to be influential only for short-term market movements. You should still depend on fundamental analysis for long-term investments, as it is a much safer bet for the investors.

To get the most out of the technical analysis indicators, we will discuss in the following sections some of the popular chart types that investors worldwide use to track price changes over time quickly.

### Line Charts

Line charts are basic charts that investors use to track the periodical change of prices for a particular financial asset. A line chart is precise and provides only essential information regarding the closing prices of an asset. All the closing prices for a day that are pointed out using a dot will be combined using a line, making it easy for the investor to understand whether the trend is an uptrend. You can use line charts to represent any kind of indicators such as support and resistance, volatility, and liquidity of the assets.

While line charts are suitable for research, they are not quite enough to make trading decisions as a day trader.

### Histogram

A histogram, also known as a bar chart, is the advanced implementation of line graphs. It provides four essential details about the asset for the investor. The histogram represents the opening price, closing price, the highest trading price, and the lowest trading price for a financial asset in a day.

*Which lines represent which?*

- **Bottom Vertical Line**

  The bottom vertical line determines a particular asset's lowest trading market price for a particular day.

- **Top Vertical Line**

  The top vertical line represents a particular asset's highest traded market price for a particular day.

- **Horizontal Lines**

  These lines represent the opening and closing prices for a particular asset for a particular day.

Histograms can also be compressed to be represented for a few hours instead of for whole trading hours.

### Candlestick Charts

Candlestick charts are the Japanese version of bar charts. They became famous with western investors due to their gripping colors and better representation of bearish and bullish trends to track market sentiment easily. Candlestick charts use green and red colors to represent the stock movement.

### Support and Resistance

Support and resistance are technical indicators that technical analysts usually use to estimate the probability of a reversal in the prevailing trend. Both support and resistance are determined by market psychology, and advanced traders use trendlines and moving averages to determine support and resistance lines efficiently.

Usually, a downtrend happens when people are pessimistic about the stock's future, which is called a bear run. During this bear run, the concentration of buying decreases, making the stock price decrease. Once the stock price reaches a specific point, bulls will start to compete with bears to raise the stock price. The trendline formed during the reversal of a downtrend is known as a support line.

In the same way, when the concentration of selling decreases, the stock price will increase, making bears compete with bulls to sell their own positions and reduce the stock price. This trendline formed during the uptrend reversal is known as the resistance line.

Usually, both bears and bulls compete for a lot of time during the market hours, making it easy for technical analysts to observe the support and resistance lines to create entry and exit points for the trade. When you follow these trendlines, place them and check past historical data and observe the market sentiment toward these trend lines.

## Bulls and Bears

Stock market movement is often decided by two enthusiastic investment groups known as bears and bulls in the market. All beginners should understand the philosophy that surrounds these groups to get the most out of the trading battles that decide the market direction.

### *What Is a Bull Market?*

Bulls are investors who believe in the economy and pump different financial assets to reach an all-time new price. Bulls believe that the companies they are investing in are trying to change the world with their innovations. A bull market also represents faith and proves that the economy is in an uptrend, increasing the number of jobs and the development index. Almost all the retail investors depending on investment as a career can be called bulls because they increase their portfolio value when the price of the individual stock prices increase.

### *What Is a Bear Market?*

Bears are investors who believe that some companies and assets are on the verge of a downtrend, and hence, they decide to get the most out of this situation by shorting their open positions and selling them back for a profit. Shorting stocks means taking money from brokers or lending stocks from other investors for a bit of interest. When the market is in a bull run, the economy cripples and recession occurs, leading to people losing jobs and companies reducing their production. The bull run will also be followed when black swan events such as the global pandemic occur.

As an investor, it is essential for you to constantly focus on the megatrends that are changing the world and how they can affect the bull-bear market directions. Artificial intelligence, work from home culture, and vaccines are some of the megatrends that are now deemed influential in 2022.

# Chapter 3: Different Types of Trading

The stock market provides different opportunities for different traders that exist. Traders from all financial markets use the trading strategies mentioned in this chapter to increase the value of their investment. Every trading strategy has its advantages and limitations. As an aspiring trader, you need to understand that retrospection is essential to decide which trading strategy to follow for the long term. Your own experience will shape your trading journey, and hence, logging all your trading activity is recommended.

Investors can trade popular financial markets such as the stock market, forex market, and cryptocurrencies with different restrictions. While the information provided in this chapter is universal, you always need to reconfirm the restrictions in your country for the financial market you are trying to invest in for a better estimation of your returns and legal concerns.

## Day Trading

A few decades back, stock markets worldwide were dominated by large financial institutions and hedge funds considered big market players. They manipulated the stock prices to help their client's value increase. However, with the inception of the internet, how people perceive the stock market has changed extensively. The growth of online brokerage and online trading has paved a path for retail investors.

Retail investors are mostly day traders who influence the market's movement by making their trading decisions based mostly on their efficiency of technical analysis. Day trading is a trading strategy where investors buy and sell shares within the end of the trading day. Day trading can be considered a profession that needs a lot of knowledge, speed, and gut instincts.

If you are looking forward to starting your investing journey by day trading, it may not be a good idea. Day trading needs at least a little bit of investing experience to get the best results. Day trading can be considered extremely risky because market volatility usually changes within minutes. Day traders also should be aware of market psychology to understand why a particular financial asset is performing well and why another is not performing well. Even with all these calculations, you can sometimes lose money because of sudden black swan events such as political scams and earthquakes that can crash the market.

Even with all these potential red flags, day trading is still considered one of the versatile professions in the ever-expanding stock market because of the enormous returns it provides for investors.

### What Does a Day Trader Do?

A day trader's primary objective is to use the volatility that always exists in the market. In a day trader timeline, the first few hours of the day are usually buying stocks that are on the rise. Until the end of the trading hours, day traders wait for sweet spots to sell their open positions for small profits. Finally, at the end of the trading day, even if there are some losses for a few positions, day traders will close them. A day trader makes a strict rule of not holding their open positions to minimize additional losses because of the events outside the trading hours.

Most of the day traders will depend on technical analysis, charts, and advanced strategies to capitalize on the small market movements during trading hours.

## Day Trading Strategies

A day trader often uses technical analysis concepts such as support and resistance lines to mark their trade's entry and exit points. However, simply depending on chart patterns and chart indicators is not enough to have consistent returns. All day traders also follow different advanced strategies to get the most out of the volatility that always exists in the market.

1. **Making Use of Analytical Software**

   Analytical software uses automatic machine learning and data analysis algorithms to predict the market movement. Many day traders use this analytical software to make their trading decisions. Analytical tools, however, need enough data to have a better probability of providing successful trade decisions.

   As a day trader, you must use this analytical software only to strengthen your already confirmed strategy. Depending entirely on computers for your investment choices is never a good idea.

2. **News Trading**

   Believe it or not, most of the time the market is controlled by events unrelated to the market. An earthquake occurring in the Middle East can reduce the stock price of Tesla. Everything is interlinked in the investment world, and you need a lot of awareness of global events to unlink them. News traders are a kind of day trader who depend entirely on news sources to make trading decisions. Many news traders also scrape the news articles that are constantly being updated by the news sources using complex software and find the most popular keywords in the trend. Once they find these keywords, they quickly connect them to many of their present stocks to make their trading decisions.

3. **Scalpers**

   Scalpers are the kind of day traders who make their trading decisions even when there are small market movements. Scalpers' main motive is to make as much profit as possible without worrying about long-term effects. Scalpers mainly depend on technical analysis factors to make their decisions.

## Swing Trading

Swing trading is a trading technique where investors hold their positions for a short period, ranging from a few weeks to a few months until they liquidate their positions for a profit. Swing trading was first used by retail investors in the early 2000s when the market was occupied by bears and when it became challenging for day traders to make profits.

The main focus of swing trading is to utilize the short-to-medium-term gains that are common within the market movement. An investor with a preference for swing trading always needs to be aware of fundamental and technical analysis to make correct judgment calls, especially when there is high volatility in the market.

The main goal of a swing trader is also to find the potential entry points in the trade, which will soon lead to a complete uptrend or downtrend. Swing traders depend on technical indicators such as MACD indicators, head and shoulder patterns, and Bollinger's bonds to see this entrance point. These are advanced candlestick chart patterns that can help you create a solid trading plan.

Not all securities in the stock market are good options for swing trading. Income stocks such as Apple and Amazon can be tough to be traded with swing trading tactics because the change in the prices is sideways for income stocks most of the time. Choose a stock with high volatility and observe the historical chart patterns to find swings that can help you estimate the next entrance and exit points for your trade.

## Position Trading

Position trading is a trading technique where the investor focuses more on the long-term asset value increase instead of depending on the assets to make quick profits. Most position traders are investors trying to save money for the future or fulfill their long-term goals. Position traders need not worry about short-term price fluctuations and any minute details related to their investment. However, just like the tremendous profit potential, a loss is also inherent with positions trading, as some stocks can fall below the purchase point and never rise again.

Use technical indicators such as the 50-day moving average to understand how your assets can perform in the long term.

## Options Trading

Options trading is one of the popular ways to trade in the stock market. The number of stock investors depending on options has increased exponentially in the past few decades. To be profitable with options, you need to estimate the correct financial asset and evaluate the time and intensity at which they are going to change. Many consider options as gambling because many people often lose money with options, especially beginners. However, like any other investment strategy, options trading can also be mastered with both knowledge and experience.

### What Are the Options?

Options are financial contracts that depend on the performance of the underlying asset. For example, if you bet on gold, then the change in the price value of gold will either increase or decrease your options contract value depending on whether the direction of the price is toward your bet or against your bet. Options contracts have both buyers and sellers, and option contract writers are always obligated to fulfill their contract terms, whereas option contract buyers are not obligated but have a choice as to whether or not to execute their contract.

Option contract writers often use them to generate passive income or to hedge their own portfolios. However, option buyers' primary goal will be to earn huge returns with their bets or even to protect their own positions.

### Components of an Option Contract

Whenever you buy an option contract for a stock you like, you need to remember three basic things.

1. You need to select the type of option contract.
2. You need to select the expiration date for the contract.
3. You need to select the strike price for the contract.
4. You need to select the premium that you are going to pay for the contract.

### Option Contract Types

Options contracts are usually of two types: Call options and Put options.

- **Call Option Contracts**

Call option contracts are options contracts that support an investor who is a bull. When you buy a call option contract, you expect that the price of a stock will increase over a particular time. So, as an investor, you make a contract emphasizing that you will be buying a set of shares for a prefixed price known as the strike price.

*Example:*

Tom is a tech enthusiast and is a smartphone geek. He has recently researched the augmented reality software that Apple will introduce to all of its users in the next update. Tom is sure that both critics and its users will receive Apple Augment technology well. Due to this, he expects that Apple shares will rise by at least $10 within the next three months. He wants to get the most out of this situation, so he decides to buy a call option contract for 100 shares with a premium of $300 for the expiration date of three months and a strike price of $70.

At the time of buying call option contracts, Apple's share price is $55, and if Apple shares cross over $70, then Tom will have profits. Now, after three months, two scenarios may happen:

1. Tom is right about the success of Apple's augmented technology. Several investors started to invest in Apple, and as a result, Apple shares raised close to $80. Tom, who bought a call options contract, now can buy 100 Apple

shares that cost $80 at only $70. With a premium of $200, Tom now has an overall profit of $800 for this options trade.

2. Tom is wrong about Apple's latest augmented technology. It did not fare well with critics and users, leading to no increase in Apple's share price. After three months, Apple shares are at $65, and the share price does not cross the strike price, making his options contracts expire worthless. As option contracts don't have any obligation, he ends with an overall loss of $200 premium amount that he paid for.

Call option contracts are primarily used by investors when they are hopeful of their future. Risks involved with call option contracts are also relatively minimal because you are not forced to buy the underlying asset with the agreed-upon price. However, if you are writing call option contracts to generate passive income, your risk can be infinite because the share value can rise as much as possible.

- **Put Option Contracts**

Put option contracts are options contracts that support an investor who is a bear. When you buy a put option contract, you expect that the price of a stock will decrease over a particular time. So, as an investor, you make a contract emphasizing that you will be buying a set of shares for a prefixed price known as the strike price.

*Example*:

Sam is an automobile enthusiast and has always rooted for electric car companies such as Tesla. He believes that electric car technology is the future and has done much research that backs his theory. He has invested most of his savings with Tesla and has made good returns over the last couple of years. He recently, however, became fearful about the future of Tesla after reading a news article that said that Apple, the most valuable company in the world, is starting to enter into the electric car industry. He became fearful because Apple would take a part of the electric car sales that Tesla has now. Even though he is not sure whether or not Apple will announce it, he decides to hedge his open positions with the put options contracts. At the time of buying put option contracts, Tesla was trading close to $300 per share. He expects that going to $260 per share is not a loss even with an Apple electric car announcement.

He buys a put option contract that secures his portfolio by paying a premium of $1,500 with a strike price of $250. So, if the Tesla share value decreases by $250, he can sell his shares for the fixed strike price of $250 within the expiration date of three months.

Now, after three months, two scenarios may happen:

1. Sam is right about his prediction. Apple announced the electric car models they are launching in the next financial year. Investors have quickly liquidated their positions in Tesla because of this announcement, and Tesla's stock

price will plummet below $250, providing profit for Sam.

2. Sam is wrong about the prediction. Apple did not announce any electric car production details for the next financial year, and hence, the stock price of Tesla did not plummet, making Sam's put option contracts worthless. He also faces a loss of $1,500 because of the premium he has paid for the put option contract owner.

Put option contracts are primarily used by investors when they doubt the company's future. Put option contracts' risks are more than the call option contracts because it is not quite common for the share prices to fall as you expect, especially when bulls dominate the market. The writer of put option contracts also holds substantial risk because they need to buy underlying assets for a lower price if the seller exercises their right.

### Expiration Date of the Contract

If the option contract's expiration date is nearer, then the value of the option contract will decrease. On the other hand, if you want to buy options contracts with an extended expiration date of as far as three years, then the premium you need to pay for it will increase.

### Strike Price of the Contract

A call option contract will usually have a strike price above the current market share price. You can also buy a call option contract at the current market price, but it will cost more. In the same way, A put option contract will usually have a strike price that is way below the current market share price. You can also buy a put option contract for the current market price, but it will cost more.

### The Premium of the Contract

You can usually trade or buy your option contracts depending on the buyer's premium to buy for the contract. If the underlying stock is less volatile, then the premium of the contracts will increase. On the other hand, if the underlying stock is more volatile, then the premium of contracts will decrease.

You can use the same option contract strategies on any financial asset apart from stocks, such as cryptocurrencies and foreign currency pairs.

## Futures Trading

Futures contracts are versatile derivative contracts that act as risk-management strategies for many businesses and investors. Unlike options contracts, where you will not have any obligation, futures contracts lock you into fulfilling the contract. Futures contracts are hence called locked derivatives. Futures contracts are mainly used by businesses that export and import commodities. Commodities run the world, and the prices of these commodities change depending on different political, social, and economic conditions.

Futures contracts are risky financial assets that can not only wipe away your investment with a wrong bet but also make you pay in return. But still, futures contracts are popular because they provide huge returns, typically five times more than regular financial contracts.

*Real-World Example:*

Let us suppose that Chin Chun, a Chinese farmer of onions, decides to harvest his 100 acres to export onions to the United States of America. Even though he is sure that his onions will be harvested well before the end of the year, he is not sure whether or not he will get his investment back because of the ongoing trade war that can increase his overall expense for selling these onions.

Chin Chun expects to have a $1,000 sale price per quintal to get profits for the hard work. So, he makes a future contract with a speculator in the international market, Jimmy. Jimmy agrees to buy a quintal of onions for $1,000 by the end of the year. Jimmy has done enough research and has concluded that there will be no trade restrictions for essential items such as onions and was therefore sure that a quintal of onions will go for more than $1,000 in the international market.

Now, by the end of the year, two scenarios may happen:

- Scenario 1: Onion prices decreases

Chin Chun was right. The latest U.S. administration has made trade restrictions with Chinese sellers, and it became difficult for Chin Chun to export his onions to the USA. Because of more supply and less demand for Chinese farmers, the export price of one quintal of onions has decreased to less than $900. As agreed upon, Jimmy buys the onions with a loss of $100, whereas Chin Chun sold nions with a profit of $100.

- Scenario 2: Onion prices increase

Jimmy was right. The latest U.S. administration doesn't make any trade restrictions with Chinese farmers, and U.S. businesses did not outsource these essential commodities from other countries. This situation made demand increase for Chinese onions, and therefore the price of onions has risen as far as $1,200. As agreed upon, Chin Chun sells the onions with a loss of $200 under the market price, whereas Jimmy buys the onions with a profit of $200.

In the same way, you can buy any other financial assets such as stocks and cryptocurrencies with the assurance of buying or selling these assets at a fixed price after some time. All financial markets use escrow-based services to make futures contracts as seamless as possible. Not everyone can start futures trading immediately because both governments and investment brokers will first ask you to deposit a sum of money to start futures trading, as this trading strategy is extremely risky.

# Dividend Investment

A dividend investment strategy is often considered the most conservative way to invest in the stock market. You will have fewer risks with dividend investing, as all the companies that provide dividends to their stockholders have consistent growth and profits.

A dividend is a financial instrument provided as a reward for the investors who are holding the open positions of a stock instead of selling them. Dividends are usually offered once or twice a year, and sometimes dividends will also be released as a surprise if there are huge profits for the company in a quarter.

## How Do I Find Better Dividend Stocks?

To find better-paying dividend stocks, you need to confirm the dividend yield ratio for that particular stock over the years. The dividend yield is the ratio percentage of the stock price received for people holding the stock over a long time.

Do thorough research about the company's performance in the recent quarters. Consistent performance is essential for companies to pay high dividend yields to their investors.

# Chapter 4: Understanding Cryptocurrencies

Cryptocurrencies are currently the talk of the town of the financial industry due to their insane return value in the last few years. Apart from the profits that cryptocurrencies can provide to you, it would be best if you also understood the philosophy surrounding them before trying to understand their impact.

## Why Are Cryptocurrencies Important?

Cryptocurrencies are the only popular decentralized financial assets available for you to invest in. All other financial assets, such as stocks, currencies, bonds, and mutual funds, are in one way or another backed and controlled by centralized institutions such as governments, banks, and financial institutions. Cryptocurrencies are also dependent on Blockchain technology, which is said to be the next big thing, like the internet.

The primary goal of cryptocurrencies is not to become an alternative to fiat currency but to provide a solution for people looking forward to escaping from the centralization they usually are a part of. Financial institutions such as banks often track your information and restrict you from making certain transactions, and cryptocurrencies don't work like that. Even though every transaction is visible, no one can track you or restrict you from conducting transactions.

Cryptocurrencies and the underlying Blockchain technology can transform the world into a much better place. This is the exact reason why many investors and financial enthusiasts are confident about the future of Bitcoin and other alternative coins. To help understand how to invest in different cryptocurrencies, you first need to understand important details about Bitcoin and the Blockchain technology that supports it.

## What Is Bitcoin?

Bitcoin is the first decentralized cryptocurrency that revolutionized a new way to spend or store money. Satoshi Nakamoto created Bitcoin in 2008, and since then it has remained the most popular digital currency. Bitcoin is entirely open-source, and you can easily find the complete source code of Bitcoin over the internet. It is built upon Blockchain technology, which is a peer-to-peer network system. The primary foundation of Bitcoin is that it maintains a public ledger of all transactions that happen in that network. Anyone can explore the transactions that happen using a website such as Blockexplorer.com.

The public ledger is quite different from the private ledger that banks and intermediary services such as Paypal use. The sole focus of these public ledgers is to solve the double spending problem.

### *What Is the Double Spending Problem?*

Imagine a digital asset such as a picture that you have taken. You can upload it to different social media platforms, and still no one will ask you further questions because it is harmless and yours. On the other hand, imagine reproducing digital currency and using them twice? It can be a serious legal offense. A picture is accepted as something that can be used twice, but this doesn't work for something financial, because money has trust with society. If anyone could double spend the digital currency, it would inspire distrust from people.

Bitcoin solves this double spending problem by using complex encryption algorithms which depend on the miners who verify all the transactions on the network.

# How Does Bitcoin Work?

Bitcoin and all the existing cryptocurrencies use a complex working model to make, verify, and embed transactions into the Blockchain network. A simple example provided below will help you understand the process that happens in the backend when someone makes a simple Bitcoin transaction.

**Real-World Scenario:**

Donny is a network and tech enthusiast who has rigorously followed the development of cryptocurrencies and the overall effect of Blockchain technology on the economy. Despite knowing a lot of theoretical stuff about cryptocurrencies, he never made an actual transaction. So, he decided to make a real-life transaction for the first time. He researched and found out that a nearby shop accepts Bitcoin as a payment option.

He immediately goes to the cafe and orders an espresso. Now, when he has to pay the bill after drinking the espresso, he scans the QR code on the bill desk, and after a few seconds, the Bitcoin transaction happens, just like all other digital transactions such as with Apple Pay. But a lot happens in the backend when a Bitcoin transaction happens.

Here are the detailed steps to help you understand the concept of cryptocurrencies in a much better way.

**Step 1:**

Donny first needs to install a cryptocurrency exchange to buy Bitcoins with fiat currency. Many famous brokers such as Binance can quickly help you buy any cryptocurrency that exists. Once you buy a cryptocurrency, an online wallet will be created for you. A wallet consists of a public and private key to store your Bitcoin safely. No one can access your wallet without a private key. It would be best to store this private key safely to access your Bitcoins. Losing this private key can make you lose your Bitcoins forever. All exchanges charge a small fee to help you convert your fiat currency into cryptocurrencies and vice versa. Different countries have different regulations about how much fiat money you can spend to buy cryptocurrencies.

**Step 2:**

When Donny scans the QR code, the wallet software will automatically convert the fiat currency rate into BTC and ask Donny to provide his authentication details so that the transaction can happen. For example, if the transaction cost is $60, then the wallet software will check the current USD-BTC transfer price to determine the number of BTC that needs to be sent to the user. Here, authentication represents Donny's private key, and without a private key, a transaction can never happen.

**Step 3:**

When Donny authenticates and processes his transaction, the transaction details will first be partially embedded into the Blockchain. During this stage, the transactions can either be canceled or not processed. Whenever you make transactions, you should make sure that they are verified. During this partial stage, nodes in the network, also known as miners, will place a bundle of transactions into a block to be verified. Different cryptocurrencies use different ways to make sure that the transactions are legit. Once the miner verifies the transactions and embed them into the distributed ledger system, it is impossible to manipulate them.

## Is Bitcoin Anonymous?

No. Bitcoin and other cryptocurrencies are not anonymous but pseudonymous. All cryptocurrencies provide transparency to the user, and hence, anyone can check the transactions associated with your public number. However, it is challenging for individuals to link Bitcoin public addresses to their real-life identities. This unique feature makes all cryptocurrencies pseudonymous.

Research based on behavior-based cluster techniques has often proven that it is difficult to trace someone's identity using their Bitcoin public address. To be on the safe side, always follow safety techniques to avoid being phished by hackers. It is also highly recommended to use encrypted web services such as TOR service while making your Bitcoin transactions.

## Centralization vs Decentralization

Before investing in cryptocurrencies, it is essential to understand the philosophy they are built upon. All financial institutes such as stock markets are decentralized because they are controlled by a higher entity such as governments or reserve banks. With centralization comes control of how you can use your earnings. While centralization is better for many things, it minimizes the freedom you have with your assets.

On the other hand, cryptocurrencies are decentralized and don't allow anyone to dictate rules in the network. A single person doesn't make decisions, and hence, there is more transparency and trust involved with all the users in the network. This philosophy is a revolutionary idea that can change the world.

# Why Should You Invest in Cryptocurrencies Such as Bitcoin?

Wall Street experts have always been divided about whether or not cryptocurrencies are a good investment choice. While volatility and environmental concerns are a drawback for cryptocurrencies, they possess many advantages, making them popular with investors.

1. **Lower Transaction Fees**

   Compared with other online payment providers, Bitcoin charges a minimal transaction fee for all the transactions, making it a probable solution. In the modern world, both credit card companies and online payment providers such as Paypal are charging high fees due to people having no other choice.

   The transaction fees collected from users will also be provided as an incentive for the miners that provide computational power to verify the transactions happening in the Blockchain network.

2. **Solve World Problems**

Satoshi Nakamoto designed Bitcoin to solve world problems. In an ideal world, every citizen should have the same opportunities. However, in reality, the world is run by corporations and is entirely controlled by a handful of people. Big players in the market have controlled politics and power-grabbing in the financial world. These market players don't worry about regular people, and hence, sometimes due to their decisions, ordinary people pay the price.

Even after incidents such as the housing bubble crisis and hyperinflation in Venezuela and Zimbabwe, centralized institutions still control us. Bitcoin and other cryptocurrencies can solve world problems, especially in underdeveloped countries where the government is highly corrupt.

Usage of Bitcoin as a transactional currency within different communities of Venezuela and South Sudan during high turmoil and political situations is a great example to understand the possibilities of Bitcoin as a preferred medium of transaction in the future.

3. **Financial Innovations**

   The financial world is constantly innovating, creating opportunities for investors by creating new assets. For example, options trading that started as a niche investment asset is now one of the preferable ways to start investing. Especially in finance, there is a lot of innovation for people to choose from. Blockchain technology, which Bitcoin is dependent on, is efficient enough to create financial innovations that are decentralized. Decentralized Finance (Defi) is a unique cryptocurrency branch that focuses majorly on these projects.

   Innovative projects that support and promote peer-to-peer lending are receiving crowdfunding and are already in the development stages.

4. **A Stable Store of Value**

   There is no advantage in assets if their value decreases with time. Even though there is unpredictability with the volatility of cryptocurrencies, most of them are still considered a great way to become valued investments. Bitcoin is probably the most popular stable cryptocurrency and has been for a long time, and it will be for the foreseeable future.

5. **Great Returns**

Cryptocurrencies provide significant returns to all their investors. When people lose money by investing in cryptocurrencies, the popular reason is always panic. Because of its decentralized nature, the value of Bitcoin is often controlled by various factors unrelated to the world economy. Sometimes, even a tweet from Elon Musk can reduce the price of Bitcoin. However, despite these flaws, Bitcoin has provided more than 1,000% returns for the investors who have believed in it for five years. With many claiming vast chances of Bitcoin reaching $100,000 very soon, extraordinary returns are always possible.

6. **Smart Contracts**

Smart contracts are like applications that depend on the Blockchain platform. Ethereum, a famous cryptocurrency, has revolutionized the smart contract industry, making many third-party developers create decentralized applications on top of it. Non-fungible tokens are also contracts that utilize the functionalities of the Ethereum network. With the innovation in smart contract technology, the popularity and value of these cryptocurrencies will also increase exponentially.

### 7. Great Community

The crypto community is very active and boasts many famous figures who support the importance of cryptocurrencies. Several CEOs such as Elon Musk and Jack Dorsey have supported cryptocurrencies openly. The crypto community is filled with intellects, investors, engineers, and scientists who believe in the future of a decentralized economy.

### 8. Blockchain Technology

When investing in cryptocurrencies, you directly support the development of Blockchain technology, which is believed to be the next stage of the internet. Blockchain technology is secure, fast, and convenient to use. Even developers mention that it is easier to work with the Blockchain ecosystem than the software industry's already existing ecosystem. Over the next few decades, there are high chances of transforming a centralized economy into a decentralized economy with the help of Blockchain technology.

# Why Should You Not Invest in Cryptocurrencies?

As with every financial investment choice, cryptocurrencies face challenges. As an investor, you need to carefully understand these factors before investing in cryptocurrencies.

1. **Uncertainty**

   The most viable reason for you to stay away from cryptocurrencies is their uncertainty. Many of the Blockchain networks are still in their initial stages and need a lot of development from hundreds of thousands of developers to achieve their vision. As people's belief in the technology often defines Bitcoin and other cryptocurrency prices, restrictions from the federal government can void many projects without a chance for further development.

2. **Misuse of Cryptocurrencies**

   Much debate goes on about the misuse of cryptocurrencies because of the pseudo-anonymity it provides. Cryptocurrencies became famous at their initial stages because of their usage by hackers on the dark web. In 2021, many reports emerged that many illegal transactions depend on Bitcoin, as it is almost impossible for the government to track these records. While decentralization provides an opportunity for innovation, there are also these problems that an investor needs to be aware of.

## Exchanges for Cryptocurrencies

If you are technically sound with Blockchain technology, you can mine your own crypto coins by becoming a node in the network to validate transactions. Many individuals followed this plan to increase their cryptocurrency investment portfolios in the initial days. However, with time, as it is intended to, all cryptocurrencies have become difficult to mine. So, if you currently don't have any existing portfolio, then you need to depend on third-party centralized cryptocurrency exchanges and brokers to start your investment journey.

All cryptocurrency exchanges only happen via the internet, unlike other financial assets where people can directly visit exchanges in person to make their trades. These cryptocurrency exchanges can help you exchange your cryptocurrency to fiat currency and from one cryptocurrency to another.

## *Types of Cryptocurrency Exchanges*

There are different kinds of cryptocurrency exchanges available for an average investor. You need to choose the one that is best for your needs.

### Centralized Cryptocurrency Exchanges

These are regulated exchanges and will ask you to provide KYC details before making any transaction. However, more than 90% of all the transactions that take place through exchanges are centralized and considered more reliable.

There are two ways to exchange cryptocurrencies using a centralized crypto exchange.

- **Crypto/Crypto Pairing**

Using this option, you can link your web wallet, such as metamask, and exchange your cryptocurrencies with any other cryptocurrency of your choice. Investors will often use stable coins such as USDT to sell or buy other cryptocurrencies quickly.

- **Fiat/Crypto Pairing**

Using this option, you can easily exchange cryptocurrencies with fiat currencies such as USD, GBP, or EUR. However, remember that the exchange rate for direct fiat currencies can be high based on the liquid of that crypto pair.

Coinbase and Binance are some of the popular centralized cryptocurrency exchanges. You have to create an account, deposit funds, and start investing in different cryptocurrencies.

### Decentralized Cryptocurrency Exchanges

Decentralized cryptocurrency exchanges provide anonymity to the investor, and hence, there will be no intermediary between the two parties. With decentralized cryptocurrency exchanges, you can only trade in crypto pairs. The problem, however, with these exchanges is the lack of security for traders because of a completely decentralized system. IDEX and Stellar DX are some of the popular decentralized cryptocurrency exchanges in the market.

Apart from exchanges, you can also use cryptocurrency brokers if you are solely speculating the price of the cryptocurrencies and their short-term changes.

## Investing in Cryptocurrencies

Investing in cryptocurrencies needs a lot of research, technical understanding, and a firm belief in the philosophy of decentralization. To invest in different cryptocurrencies, you need to go through a two-stage process.

- **Research**

The first stage always is about how much you know about the architecture and goals of the cryptocurrency project. You can also use financial metrics to understand the growth potential of a cryptocurrency.

- **Accumulation**

Once you have a handful of choices to choose from, you need to select a bunch of cryptocurrencies so that your portfolio will be diversified. Use market metrics to position the size of different cryptocurrencies you have already invested in. Accumulation also involves choosing different technical analysis indicators.

As an investor, you also need to be aware of different analysis philosophies that can help you to estimate the market movements.

1. **Fundamental Analysis**

   Using this analysis, investors will research Blockchain and cryptocurrency information using several factors, such as volatility, to decide whether or not they are a worthwhile investment choice.

2. **Technical Analysis**

   Using this analysis, investors will use charts and chart indicators to look at the past price trends and link them to the current market price trends and make decisions.

3. **Sentimental Analysis**

   Using this analysis, the investors will closely follow the market forecasts and use investors' sentiment about a particular cryptocurrency to judge the performance and movement of the cryptocurrencies.

4. **Capital Analysis**

   Using this analysis, the investors will depend solely on their risk-management strategies to judge the performance of their portfolios.

To invest in cryptocurrencies, you can follow several strategies, just like in the stock market. To choose which of the following mentioned below is entirely a personal preference.

Before choosing, we want you to follow the below-mentioned checklist to decide which strategy works best for you.

- Use paper trading to experiment with different kinds of trading strategies.
- Every strategy has its advantages and disadvantages. Most of the time, these will change according to the investor involved.
- Your choice of investment strategy will also change according to the commitments you currently have in your life. For example, if you have a day job, it becomes impossible to be a day trader.

Here are some of the popular cryptocurrency strategies available to an average trader.

1. **Day Trader**

   A day trader is an investor who uses the extreme volatility present in the cryptocurrency market for their benefit. All day traders will sell their open positions of cryptocurrencies by the end of the trading day. As a day trader, you need to focus more time on technical indicators to exit and enter the trade. For better trades as a day trader, you also need to closely follow different cryptocurrency news sources and influential persons in the industry, as they are significant to the price movement in the industry.

2. **Position Trader**

   A position trader is a cryptocurrency investor who optimizes over long-term investment choices. Being a volatile market, this needs an extreme skillset to judge the cryptocurrencies that can perform in the long run. As a position trader, you should not worry about short-term price fluctuations and panic sell at any time. Hold as long as you can to get better returns.

3. **Swing Trader**

   A swing trader is a cryptocurrency investor who observes market swings to make trading decisions. These swings are usually formed because of excessive buying or selling of open positions over an extended period. Usually, prominent market players liquidate their positions without attracting any market attention. Swing traders make use of these swings to their advantage and make quick returns.

4. **Index Trader**

Index trading is a brand new cryptocurrency strategy where the investors need to estimate the market movement of many cryptocurrencies instead of just one cryptocurrency. When you are grouping cryptocurrencies, make sure that you include a diversified portfolio for better results.

5. **Scalpers**

Scalping is a complex trading skill that can provide fruitful results for a cryptocurrency investor. To be a scalper, you need to be aware of different technical analysis indicators and chart patterns to judge concise term price movements. Understanding different candlestick chart patterns is also crucial for scalping efficiently.

6. **Derivatives Trading**

Like in the stock markets, cryptocurrencies provide derivatives for investors to hedge their positions. As the owner of the options contract, you can exercise it or not according to the conditions. Many cryptocurrency investors also invest in futures trading for quick gains. However, it is not recommended for beginners to try futures or forwards trading because of the uncertainty it involves.

## Important Fundamental Analysis Factors

To invest in cryptocurrencies, you need to be aware of some of the financial metrics related to cryptocurrencies while researching your investment.

1. **Transaction Count**

   By using this metric, you will find the number of daily transactions in the Blockchain network. The number of transactions is directly proportional to the popularity of the cryptocurrency and describes how active the community is.

2. **Active Addresses**

   If many addresses are not active in a Blockchain network, it is not a good sign for an investor. Active addresses describe that people are constantly using the network as a transaction medium.

3. **Mining Cost**

   Mining cost describes the competition that is there to validate the transactions. When there is a high mining cost, it describes that many transactions are happening in the network, which means a bright future for the cryptocurrency network.

4. **Hash Power**

   Hash power is a cryptographic algorithmic component that increases the difficulty rate used for mining transactions. When the hash power increases, the network's security increases, making it an efficient blockchain network.

5. **Team**

   Before investing, it is also recommended to know specific details about the founders and the developers working for the project. Most of the time, the cryptocurrency project developers will be anonymous, but many altcoin developers are transparent about their share in the network.

# Chapter 5: Investing in Altcoins

Bitcoin is the cryptocurrency that initiated the Blockchain revolution and has helped millions of retail investors understand the importance of decentralization. However, like all good things, Bitcoin, too, has become a pretty costly investment for most beginners with a bit of capital. In 2021, Bitcoin was raised as far as $60,000, making it one of the most expensive financial assets in the financial world. Bitcoin is an economic revolution and one of the few financial assets that helped pave a pathway for several other cryptocurrencies that are focusing on Blockchain technology to create real-world applications. Ethereum is one of these popular cryptocurrencies that helped developers dream about creating an alternative to Bitcoin.

All these cryptocurrencies that are not Bitcoin are called Altcoins in the cryptocurrency sphere. Altcoins hold a superior value for an investor because it involves less cost to purchase them. Altcoins also have more growth percentage when compared to Bitcoin because of new investors jumping on the bandwagon. However, it is also essential to understand that Altcoins can be a risky investment compared to Bitcoin due to their volatility.

Learning about some of the popular altcoins in the market and knowing how to create a trading strategy for these Altcoins can be a valuable investment technique for beginners and experienced investors alike.

## Ethereum

Ethereum is the second most popular cryptocurrency both in popularity and market value. The success of Ethereum is primarily due to its ability to help developers create decentralized applications on Ethereum Blockchain. Imagine it as an app store for decentralized applications that use the technicalities of Blockchain. The success of Ethereum is due to enthusiastic developers who depend on Ethereum to create real-world applications for different uses. For example, NFTs that are the talk of the town in the financial world mainly depend on the Ethereum Blockchain.

The native token of Ethereum is called Ethernet (ETH), and when you invest in Ethereum using a broker, you will usually be holding Ether in your cryptocurrency wallet. Ethereum is transforming from a proof-of-work consensus algorithm to a proof-of-stake consensus algorithm to verify all the transactions.

### *What Are Decentralized Applications (Dapps)?*

Ethereum made it possible for developers to interact with the core Blockchain technology by publishing smart contracts. A smart contract is just a programming instruction by the developer to perform a task on the Blockchain. A set of smart contracts usually create a decentralized application, also known as Dapps, for real-world users. In exchange for using the Ethereum Blockchain to perform these actions, all developers need to provide a gas fee with Ether for miners.

While Bitcoin has risen as a cryptocurrency that can be used as an exchange value, Ethereum has been promoted as a cryptocurrency that can maintain a programmable network. While both Bitcoin and Ethereum differ in their philosophies, they are decentralized, and investors expect a bright future ahead.

Due to the immense popularity of Ethereum, several online service vendors started to accept Ethereum as payment along with Bitcoin.

### *What Are Smart Contracts?*

The growing popularity of Ethereum Blockchain is primarily because of its smart contracts feature. Smart contracts are code that can automatically run on a Blockchain platform whenever a few predetermined conditions are met. All the smart contracts in the Ethereum platform are written using the Solidity language, and they use a simple "if/when...then..." statement structure to create triggers.

The success of smart contracts is mainly because they provide trust for both parties involved in a transaction. By providing trust, they eliminate intermediaries for any financial transaction. As every transaction record is embedded into the Blockchain, none of the transactions can be reversed in any way.

*Example:*

For example, we all know about sports betting platforms. All these sports betting platforms have a centralized authority, and hence, all the transactions made from these platforms are controlled by a centralized authority, making it a problem for all the users. You can be banned from making any transactions for different reasons. Decentralized smart contracts solve this problem by automatically executing your transactions without foul play from both sides.

At present, Ethereum is still a developing project. However, within the next 10 years, Ethereum is expected to become one of the more ambitious projects in the world that will have the power to fight with centralized institutions and governments.

## Cardano

Cardano is another ambitious cryptocurrency project that allows developers to create smart contracts. It is considered a third-generation cryptocurrency, and most of its hype is because of the "proof of stake" consensus algorithm it depends on.

With cryptocurrencies, there is always a problem with energy consumption that happens while validating the Blockchain transactions. Cardano uses a randomized stake algorithm to reduce energy consumption. Due to this reason, it is hailed as one of the groundbreaking green cryptocurrencies worldwide.

Cardano is also popular with investors because of its approach to research-backed Dapp development. Cardano's whitepaper was first created after rigorous research of Blockchain technologies and was peer-reviewed by hundreds of computer scientists worldwide before it was made accessible to investors. In the crypto world, where there is oftentimes less research backup for public projects, Cardano is more reliable.

The Native token of Cardano is $ADA and is currently still at a testing stage. Blockchain experts believe that Cardano can beat Ethereum because of its advanced smart contracts functionality.

# Ripple

Ripple is a centralized cryptocurrency with a philosophy that is often misunderstood by Blockchain experts. Unlike other cryptocurrencies, Ripple is not a decentralized project controlled by a company known as Ripple Technologies. However, the native token $XRP has enormous investment potential despite being centralized.

The reason for the success of Ripple is its ability to make foreign transactions easily. Many banks and private institutions have already started to depend on the Ripple ecosystem to make overseas transactions instead of relying on the decades-old banking system.

### *How Does Ripple Work?*

To help you understand why Ripple is a lot more efficient than traditional bank transactions, let us discuss an example foreign transaction.

When you book a transaction from the United States to Russia using your bank, it usually takes a lot of time to transfer into the recipient's account because different countries use different banking algorithms to line up these transactions. Sometimes, your funds may even disappear due to glitches, and it can take a lot of time to track them. These problems usually slow transaction rates for corporations and individuals, apart from dealing with fluctuations in currency prices.

Ripple is a Blockchain project that uses its network to make high-end transactions within very little time. Ripple uses node-to-node transactions as mentioned below to make these transactions.

For example, if a corporation in the USA sends 100 million USD to a corporation in Japan, the 100 million USD will first be converted into the Ripple network's native token known as XRP. Once the fiat currency is converted into XRP, the Blockchain transaction will be sent to the network and validated on one of the 41 independent servers controlled by Ripple Networks. These network nodes will verify the transaction and add the transaction details to the network.

Once the transaction is validated, the native token XRP will again be converted into fiat currency and sent to the receiver's account. Ripple charges a small transaction fee for validating the transaction. Thousands of banks and corporations have already started to use Ripple, making it the third most popular cryptocurrency in terms of market capitalization after Bitcoin and Ethereum.

## Chainlink

Usually, web and mobile applications use APIs to extract dynamic data from different sources to display for their users. Static data can be tedious and may not serve a significant purpose in real-world project implementation. Chainlink is a Blockchain project that provides dynamic data for Blockchain-centric decentralized applications.

Chainlink makes this data gathering possible with the help of trusted nodes known as Oracles. Oracles receive a part of the transaction to exchange the data in the form of native token LINK. Chainlink is still, however, a new Blockchain technology project. Many financial enthusiasts predict that when the number of decentralized applications increases, technologies such as Chainlink will also increase in tandem.

*Example Project:*

For example, if a developer decides to create a decentralized betting application, he needs real-time score alerts to make the betting platform popular with the users. Oracles in the Chainlink network will provide these real-time sources and charge a transaction fee for every request fulfilled by them.

The project founders have also mentioned that they will penalize the nodes when they send any false information to the requests received, providing developers with a unique way to obtain reliable data for their decentralized applications.

## Binance Coin

Binance Coin is also one popular Altcoin, and is increasing in value with time. It was created by Binance, one of the most trusted cryptocurrency exchanges worldwide. The main goal of the Binance coin that is supported by its Blockchain network is to help make transactions in the Binance ecosystem much better. With the help of Binance coin, users can now easily exchange cryptocurrencies using a moderate centralized provider.

As an investor, it is essential to understand the ethical concerns that surround Binance Coin. Many crypto enthusiasts believe that Binance is trying to centralize the core philosophy of crypto coins with its feasibility to grab the market share of real-world transactions. However, the CEO of Binance has shielded these claims by saying that Binance always supports the core decentralization Bitcoin and Altcoins strive for. It is right now the sixth most popular cryptocurrency according to market capitalization.

## Dogecoin

Dogecoin is one of the many cryptocurrencies that arrived as a joke in the initial days of the cryptocurrency boom. Dogecoin became popular when Elon Musk, the CEO of Tesla, promoted it on Twitter. Dogecoin is one of the most popular cryptocurrencies when judged by market capitalization.

It has an unlimited supply, and hence, many financial enthusiasts judge it as a lousy investment choice due to the chances of hyperinflation. It uses a scrypt algorithm developed by Litecoin developers to verify the transactions. It is also more scalable than Litecoin, making it a strong investment choice for individuals with less capital.

## How Do I Invest in Altcoins?

Alternative cryptocurrencies, also known as Altcoins, are cryptocurrencies that are not Bitcoin. Almost all of them depend on Blockchains technology but may vary in the consensus mechanism that they use. All Altcoins' prices in some way or other depend on the cost of Bitcoin. By the end of 2021, Altcoins already occupied more than 60% of the cryptocurrency market. The success of meme coins such as Dogecoin has helped boost the demand for Altcoins and made a potential money-making machine for individuals with very little capital to invest in traditional investment methods.

Most of the Altcoins depend on smart contracts technology to make their revenue. Not all Altcoins are decentralized, either. For example, Ripple, a famous Altcoin, is a centralized cryptocurrency. Individual research is essential for getting the most out of your investment with Altcoins.

As of now, even though the price of these Altcoins follows the trajectory of Bitcoin, many financial enthusiasts believe that with time, these Altcoins are capable of creating their ecosystem and providing fruitful results for all the investors involved.

The proof of work algorithm that Bitcoin uses has been controversial right from its inception because of the enormous energy consumption it involves. Many Altcoins are now depending on the proof of stake consensus algorithm to validate transactions.

However, as the Altcoins market is often overwhelmed with many options, you need to have a clear strategy and vision to execute your trades as an investor. There are also an overwhelming number of options for you to explore in the Altcoins market, and therefore it is highly suggested not to invest in any Altcoins that don't already have growing popularity within the crypto community.

To invest in Altcoins, you need to create a different trading strategy suitable to your needs. We are providing a strategy that will help you determine the best cryptocurrencies available and how to diversify your investment portfolio.

1. **Perform Research**

   Strong research is essential to understand the motive of a cryptocurrency in the long run. Without a clear vision, there are very few chances of a cryptocurrency becoming successful in the future. While researching, you need to focus on fundamental analysis factors such as market capitalization, volume, volatility, liquidity, and the trend of prices.

2. **Check Different Metrics**

   Many technical metrics can help you judge the popularity and sustainability of a cryptocurrency. Use online tools and APIs to extract technical information about the cryptocurrency you have chosen automatically. You can also use automatic scraping tools to extract metrics such as number of coins, number of transactions, and the mining reward for transactions to understand the popularity of the Altcoin.

3. **Invest Only if There Is Less Volatility and More Liquidity**

   Both volatility and liquidity are the most important metrics that you need to focus on before judging the performance of an Altcoin. Volatility determines the change in cryptocurrency prices, whereas liquidity represents the number of coins available to sell or buy immediately. If the Altcoin has less volatility and more liquidity, then it is a safe bet to invest in it.

Just like to buy Bitcoin, you need to create an account in one of the cryptocurrency brokers to get hold of these Altcoins quickly. You can also participate in ICOs to invest in the initial tokens for new cryptocurrency projects.

1. **Identify a Platform**

   First of all, it is not so easy to find cryptocurrency platforms that provide Altcoins in exchange for fiat currency. Do plenty of research, as there are many scams in the market right now. As these platforms are often decentralized, you need to depend on user experience reviews to choose a broker for your trades.

2. **Create an Account**

   When you create an account, you need to provide KYC compliance details to the broker.

Once your account is verified, you can always use Ethereum or stable coins such as USDT to buy different Altcoins.

### 3. Use Wallets Such as Metamask

Whenever you buy Altcoins, immediately transfer their details to secure online wallets like Metamask. With Metamask, you can organize different Altcoins that you have invested in without worrying about losing your private keys to hackers.

# Chapter 6: NFTs and ICOs

Collectible art is one of the most luxurious investment strategies that has bought huge returns for many investors in the last century. Collectible art involves the exchange of the original art piece or item, and it is usually challenging for retail investors to invest in rare collectible items from the internet. Due to these limitations, for many years, collectible art became an investment strategy that is only possible for rich people. With the popularity of Blockchain technology, the concept of NFTs that was first used in 2014 has provided an easy way to protect intellectual property and allow individuals to sell the ownership for a digital or physical item with just a few clicks. In 2021, the NFT market quadrupled its market value, and many investors expect NFTs to emerge as a new financial market in the next couple of years.

## What Is an NFT?

NFT is known as a Non-Fungible Token. An NFT provides a cryptographic way to determine the ownership of a digital item. A unique token is embedded into the Blockchain whenever an NFT is created in a Blockchain such as Ethereum. The token of the NFT will usually contain a unique token number, metadata describing the details of the item that the NFT is created for, and the details of ownership.

In general, all cryptocurrencies have the same value and act as transaction items. For example, Bitcoin has tokens that are fungible, and hence, they can be easily exchanged. NFTs, on the other hand, have a token that is unique and therefore holds a value for a digital item. Most NFTs are created on the Ethereum platform, and ERC-721 of the Ethereum development has made NFTs possible by introducing non-fungible tokens in the Ethereum Blockchain. As of 2021, most of the NFTs traded are embedded into the Ethereum Blockchain.

### *Characteristics of an NFT*

When you buy an NFT, you will only gain ownership of a particular digital asset and not the physical copy. Anyone can easily download a copy of the SpongeBob meme template from the internet, but only the owner of the NFT will have ownership rights to it.

1. **It Can Be Exchanged**

   Remember that the ownership rights of an NFT can be traded just like a rare collectible item. All you have to do is start a bid using one of the NFT platforms on the internet. However, remember that no two individuals can hold ownership of an NFT at one time. The owner of the NFTs will receive a small percentage of the royalties each time an NFT is exchanged.

2. **They Are Unique**

   NFTs are popular because they have a unique token and will be available only as a digital certificate in different Blockchain networks. As it is easy to prove ownership with digital assets, its value will be consistent most of the time.

3. **They Are Indivisible**

   NFTs are also indivisible, and hence the ownership for a digital asset cannot be bought by a group of people.

## *How Do I Invest in NTFs?*

As NFT investing is a new way to invest, many shady websites are trying to manipulate investors into buying NFTs of no value. Like any research that happens before an asset, investors should also complete research about both the NFT owner and the NFT auction platform to understand the asset's actual value.

1. **Choose an NFT Auction Website**

   Many websites are now trying to sell NFTs for different digital assets. Most of these auction websites provide details such as NFT, NFT creator name, and the base price for the auction.

You can provide your preferred auction value for the NFT within the auction end date. If you win the auction, you will immediately become the sole owner of the NFT, and the token will be updated with the ownership details.

2. **Use Platforms and Social Media to Trade**

   Once you get ahold of an NFT, as an investor, you need to wait some time for the NFT to increase in value and then trade it. To trade an NFT, you first need to create an auction with your desired starting amount. To get better auction offers for your NFT, try to promote it in your social media handles and advertise it to people collecting NFTs. Both networking and marketing can help your auction reach enthusiastic collectors.

3. **Do Research**

   Like any financial asset, you must conduct thorough research before investing in an NFT. Instead of buying NFTs that are rare and considered antique, buy NFTs popular with other enthusiasts. You can use Python scrapers to collect data from auction websites and APIs about the most popular niches in NFTs.

4. **Hold for a Long Time**

   Just like art pieces, NFTs will also increase in value with time. It is best to hold them as long as possible instead of selling them for quick profits. Scalping is not a good idea with NFTs, and long-term investment should be your choice for better returns.

NFTs are next-generation assets that have the potential to change the world. NFTs are still new, and hence, there are a lot of scams that are happening right now in the cryptocurrency market. Before investing, we suggest you consult a professional for better overall results.

## ICOs

Initial Coin Offerings (ICOs) are equivalent to IPOs from the stock market, and their main focus is to generate the initial capital required for the project. Right from their inception, ICOs have provided significant returns for investors involved. Ethereum, the second most popular cryptocurrency, started as an ICO project and has provided more than 2,000% returns to the stakeholders involved. These returns, compared to Wall Street returns, come because of publicly traded companies.

With these high returns, ICOs have also earned a bad reputation as people lose money after investing in ICOs that are just outright scams. The intensity with which scams have arisen made different countries create regulations for ICOs. Irrespective of these cryptocurrencies, there is still a great demand for ICOs worldwide. As an investor, your main task, however, is to be aware of the authenticity of the project.

### *How Do ICOs Work?*

ICOs are only allowed to be created for projects that depend on Blockchain technology. All the ICOs need to follow a strict pattern before making them public to distribute tokens and earn initial capital. However, one major flaw with ICOs is that they don't allow you to buy these initial tokens with fiat currencies. To invest in any ICO, you first need to convert your fiat currency to a cryptocurrency such as Bitcoin or Ethereum.

*Who Are the Participants in ICOs?*

Fundamentally, there are three participants in the ICO process.

1. ICOs are filled with projects by business startups that depend on Blockchain technology to create real-world applications for users worldwide.

2. Investors who want to make returns by investing in a project and helping them achieve their vision.

3. Centralized ICO providers who link up both investors and startups to generate capital.

4. Escrow services that act as a middleman to make sure that the collected capital is utilized correctly by the founders of the ICO.

## *Step by Step ICO Procedure*

From 2018, ICOs have become stricter due to the regulations made by different countries to minimize people losing money to baseless cryptocurrency projects. Like IPOs, different sets of procedures need to be completed before listing the project for capital generation.

*Step 1: Announcement*

First of all, the project founders need to announce their project using one of the many online forums filled with cryptocurrency projects. If people are excited about the project, then these founders will start to create a whitepaper detailing the project initiative and how the tokens will be distributed.

In this step, the project's founders will be able to take recommendations from the community to make improvements to their project.

### What should the whitepaper contain?

The whitepaper is the most critical factor for any investor to look at before investing in an ICO.

An ICO whitepaper usually will consist of:

- The description of the project.
- How the project will be implemented.
- How many stages there are in the project.
- Who the leading project developers for the project are.
- How the initial tokens will be distributed to the community.
- How many tokens will be issued.
- Details about the escrow service that will be holding the project capital.

*Step 2: Campaign and Sale*

Once the announcement is completed, the founders will announce a set of dates for investors to buy their tokens from one of the centralized ICO providers they chose to make their ICO happen. Most of the time, if there is a considerable demand for an ICO, then the ICO process will occur on a first-come, first-serve basis.

Before the time for the sale, the ICO founders need to rigorously conduct PR for their campaign to help the general public understand the necessity for their Blockchain project. Giving magazine interviews, social media, and email marketing can also help reach more crypto enthusiasts. Some ICO projects also use public figures and social media influencers to promote their project.

On the day of the sale, the investors need to exchange cryptocurrencies such as Bitcoin for native tokens. These ICO tokens have more value and often can be sold in all popular cryptocurrency exchanges.

# Chapter 7: Cryptocurrency Mining

Cryptocurrency mining can be a great passive income strategy for investors enthusiastic about cryptocurrencies. Even though there is an initial budget you need to have to start making money with cryptocurrency mining, it is still considered profitable. However, remember that you need to have a high-speed internet bandwidth, continuous power supply, and a high-end mining rig to make better returns.

## How Does Cryptocurrency Mining Work?

All Blockchain-supported cryptocurrencies depend on miners to validate the transactions in their network. Without validating transactions, there is no way to make the transactions legitimate. Without miners, most cryptocurrencies will lose their value. Miners solve mathematical problems to validate the transactions and embed them into the Blockchain network once they are sure they are legit. How these transactions can be validated is called a consensus mechanism. Proof of work and proof of stake are two popular algorithms for different cryptocurrencies available.

Your cryptocurrency network should support the Proof of Work (POW) consensus algorithm to generate passive income by mining. Bitcoin is still the most popular cryptocurrency being mined all around the world.

### *How Does the Proof of Work Algorithm Work?*

To become a miner in the Blockchain network, you first need to join the network and provide your consensus to validate the transactions. When you provide your consent, a nearly 300GB file will be downloaded into your system, and this file will consist of all the transactions that ever happened in the network.

After joining, the miner will wait for transactions to come and add them into blocks. Once the transactions are added into a block, they need to wait for the consensus from other nodes in the network to start verifying a transaction. Cryptocurrency algorithms decide to use a random algorithm to choose who should mine the next block.

You need to provide your computational power to solve complex hashing algorithms for the block present when you get your chance. Once the mathematical problem is solved, you will again send this information to nodes in the network for their approval. Once the consensus is approved, your block will be appended to the Blockchain, and all the transactions inside it will be validated. After validation, within a few hours, you will receive a reward for your contribution to maintaining the distributed ledger network.

### *Mining Hardware*

All miners need to have specific hardware to become a network node and validate transactions. At the initial stages of the Bitcoin mining revolution, the consensus and hashing algorithm was simple to crack, making it easy for individuals to mine Bitcoin right from their laptops themselves. However, Satoshi Nakamoto has designed Bitcoin mining algorithms to become complex if the competition increases. He decided to make it that way to limit the supply and control inflation of the number of Bitcoins present in the network. This theory is known as Bitcoin halving.

Bitcoin mining also became popular when some crypto enthusiasts ported a way to mine using GPUs that gamers usually use for high-end graphics. Within a few years, miners started to use it to earn some passive income. In recent years, however, Bitcoin mining with GPUs became impractical due to the complexity of the hashing algorithms. Instead of GUIs, miners now depend on a separate hardware machine known as ASICs to mine cryptocurrencies.

Application Specific Integrated Circuits (ASICs) are designed especially for mining, and hence they are more efficient as mining rigs. Because of the enormous profits that ASCIs provide, many individuals started to create mining farms, where many mining rigs are present to increase the chances of mining a block. Mining, even though it validates the transactions of the most major decentralized network globally, has recently been receiving a lot of criticism due to the chip shortage that occurred and the environmental concerns it causes.

### Mining and Environmental Impact

In 2021, Elon Musk, the CEO of Tesla, tweeted, saying that Tesla is withdrawing their decision to use Bitcoin as a transaction medium, quoting the environmental concerns. Immediately, the value of Bitcoin and other cryptocurrencies plummeted, losing more than 30% of their value within a few days. Irrespective of how thriving the cryptocurrency industry is, people are still not okay with miners consuming as much as a country's electricity to validate the transactions.

To avoid these controversies and provide a different way to validate transactions, proof of stake algorithms have been introduced by cryptocurrencies such as Cardano. These cryptocurrencies are known as green crypto coins and use a pseudo-process to randomly select a slot member to validate the transaction by staking native tokens.

## *How Do I Start Making Money With Mining?*

To make money with mining, you also need to use mining software, in addition to owning mining hardware. Mining software helps you quickly connect to a network and start mining immediately to earn money. There are many mining software out there, but we will discuss NiceHash, a popular alternative to traditional mining.

With NiceHash, you can earn money by mining with gaming rigs with AMD or Nvidia graphic cards. Of course, mining with Bitcoin is not possible with the NiceHash program, and you can only mine several popular Altcoins that provide excellent returns for miners.

### How Does NiceHash Work?

NiceHash provides an easy way to sell your computer hashing power to miners who are outsourcing the hashing power in a marketplace. When you provide your hashing power, the miner will validate the transactions, and when a reward is given to him by the Blockchain algorithm, they will automatically send your portion of the reward into your Bitcoin wallet. Most of the time, your reward will be sent to BTC. However, the newer Beta versions of NiceHash are testing to implement the integration of other Altcoins such as Ethereum and Cardano as rewards for the users.

NiceHash automatically provides the popular mining algorithms according to your hardware requirements, and hence, the time generally spent on research can be avoided with software such as NiceHash. The catch, however, is that NiceHash will charge a small part of your rewards for their services.

## How Do I Start Using Nicehash?

To start using NiceHash as it is intended, you need to follow the set of instructions that are provided below.

- **Register An account**

  To use the NiceHash software, you need to create an account from the official website. When you create an account, a private cryptocurrency wallet will be automatically made for you to withdraw your rewards. You can also link your own private BTC wallet if you want to during this step.

- **Download Software**

  Once you have registered your account, you will be redirected to a page to download the software, depending on your operating system. You need to download the latest 2.0 version if your GPU is an Nvidia graphics card or the legacy version if your GPU is an AMD-supported graphics card. Accept the license agreements during the installation so that the software can automatically install default components that are necessary for cryptocurrency mining in the background.

Once the installation is completed, enter your account details and create a worker account for you to start mining. Your worker account can be synced with other devices to your account, and this feature helps you easily track your rewards from one account if you are using multiple mining rigs.

- **Benchmark Your Device**

  Once your account is set and the software components are downloaded, you need to benchmark your device to let the NiceHash software automatically determine the mining protocols best suited for your hardware equipment. Select the precise option in the menu to improve your hash rate, memory, and clock speed.

  Once your benchmark is completed, you can now enter the start button to share your computing power with other miners in the network. You can use advanced Nvidia graphics settings to tweak the efficiency of your GPU so that memory clock speeds will be increased.

### *Proof of Stake*

Proof Of Stake is set to become the most popular consensus algorithm within the next 10 years in the crypto community. While the end goal of every consensus algorithm is to validate the transactions and embed blocks into the Blockchain, proof of stake algorithms use fewer computing resources, making it a favorable way for many Blockchain platforms to validate their distributed ledger systems.

Unlike cryptocurrency mining, staking involves staking one's own native tokens to check blocks of transactions and add to a Blockchain network. In a staking mechanism, the nodes which stake their coins and wait for their turn to validate transactions are known as validator nodes. When you stake your coins, they will be locked and released some time after the verification of the transaction.

Choosing one validator from many validators in the network is based on a randomized algorithm that depends on many factors such as the amount of stakes, age of the validator, and number of times the validator has been selected.

Cardano, Tezos, and Algorand are some of the many popular Blockchain networks that use the proof of stake mechanism as their default consensus mechanism. Several influential cryptocurrency platforms such as Ethereum have updated their codebase to migrate from the proof of work consensus mechanism to the proof of stake consensus mechanism.

# Chapter 8: Advanced Investment Opportunities

Investing in stock markets is complex and challenging, as you need a lot of research skills and patience. Not everyone has the resources to master the art of researching using both fundamental and technical analysis to find the best stocks that are performing well or can perform well in the future. It is essential for most teens who are just starting with their investing journey to depend on professionals to do research for them and to find some of the best-performing stocks they can invest in.

## Mutual Funds

Mutual funds are the most popular financial assets in the United States and most parts of the world. Mutual funds are versatile and require less research when compared to other financial assets that exist out there. Many mutual fund firms also provide consistent returns for all their investors.

A mutual fund is usually a financial strategy where a pool of money collected from different investors will be used to invest in stocks, commodities, currency pairs, and bonds after sufficient research is performed by the fund managers. A fund manager usually will have a lot of experience with different financial institutions and conduct many fundamental analyses before deciding on the assets that the pool of money will be invested in. Usually, most mutual fund firms depend on stocks and bonds to provide consistent returns to their customers. However, in the last few years, due to the enormous popularity of cryptocurrencies, many mutual funds also started to offer mutual funds that list Bitcoin and other Altcoins.

For their research work, all mutual fund firms will charge a portion of your earnings as a fee. Mutual funds can be called mild risk investment choices for an investor.

### *Why Choose Mutual Funds Over Stocks?*

The most probable reason for investing in mutual funds instead of directly investing in stocks is the highly volatile nature of individual stocks. Investing directly in stocks can be highly risky if you have not done enough research.

1. **Mutual Funds Are More Diversified**

   When you invest in stocks, you need to invest all your money in a handful of stocks. Even if you want to invest a small portion in various stocks, it becomes incredibly tedious to track all their performance. With mutual funds, all you need to do is track your overall portfolio value.

2. **Fewer Commissions**

   Even though you need to pay a small fee to the firm that provides you with a fund manager, you will be saving a lot of commission fees that you may otherwise need to pay to a stockbroker. All these stockbrokers can be highly unreliable when there is high traffic in a transaction. Investing in mutual funds is the best idea to reinvest easily. All you need to do is select an option on your mutual fund firm's interface to reinvest your earnings for compound earnings automatically.

3. **Provides Transparency**

   All mutual fund firms will also provide high transparency to all their customers. You will see what stocks your fund manager is investing the pooled money in. With transparency, you can check whether or not an investment choice is working for you efficiently.

### *Different Types of Mutual Funds*

There will be tens of investment choices for investors if they want to invest in mutual funds. The number of choices that an investor can get will also vary according to the firm they are investing in.

1. **Equity Funds**

   Equity funds are probably the most popular and readily available mutual fund type for all investors. When you invest in an equity fund, your money will automatically be invested in publicly traded companies traded in the stock market. Most of the time, you will have the option to select the type of industries that you want to invest in. For example, if you choose the large cup funds options while investing, all your money will be invested in companies with a market value of more than 10 billion.

2. **Bond Funds**

   A bond is a financial instrument where a pool of money will be invested on debts taken by governments and multinational companies. The advantage of bonds is that they are less volatile than the financial assets that usually are available to investors. It is also challenging for individuals to invest in bonds directly, and hence, if you are interested in investing with bonds, joining a mutual fund is a better option. You can choose whether to invest in government bond funds or corporate bond funds while investing. It is usually recommended to depend on government funds for more consistent returns.

3. **Hybrid Funds**

   Hybrid funds are a kind of mutual fund where your investment will be pooled for investing in a mix of financial instruments such as stocks, currency pairs, bonds, and cryptocurrencies.

***How Do I Start Investing?***

To start investing in a mutual fund, you first need to do proper due diligence about the firm you are investing in. Once you are sure that the firm can be trusted, fulfill all the KYC requirements required for creating an account. Once your account is created, deposit your money and transfer it to a fund to lock your investment for a particular time. Remember that you can withdraw your funds anytime for most mutual funds, unlike CDs, where your investment will be locked for a specific time.

## ETFs

Exchange-traded funds are a unique financial instrument where you can invest in a particular financial index, commodity, or sector instead of selecting a few companies. To be precise, an ETF trades like a stock but acts like a mutual fund. For example, if you are sure that the automobile industry will be booming in the next few months, you can select an automobile ETF that tracks all the companies present in the automobile industry. The significant advantage of ETFs is that they are more diversified and it is easier to sell your funds, unlike mutual funds. On the other hand, ETFs are also relatively riskier than mutual funds, and the investor should solely do all the research.

As they are traded like stocks, all ETFs have a commission that needs to be paid to the brokers and exchanges. As they are pooled like mutual funds, ETFs also exist in different types. Each ETF has a unique objective, and therefore sufficient fundamental analysis is recommended for efficient results. Most ETFs depend on a group of similar stocks, indexes, or sectors.

### *Different Types of ETFs*

There are hundreds of ETFs available for an investor from different exchanges. As an investor, you need to be aware of some popular ETFs that provide better returns for an investor.

- **Bond ETFs**

  Bonds are debt instruments that investors can exchange. They provide decent income to the investors and can be of different types, such as government bonds, corporate bonds, and municipal bonds. ETFs track a set of these debt instruments for a discounted price of the actual bond price. All bonds have a maturity date, after which their value will expire. On the other hand, bond ETFs don't hold a maturity value and can be easily exchanged for a profit.

- **Stock ETFs**

  A stock ETF will hold many stocks that track the performance of a sector or industry. With ETFs, you can also track the performance of a group of foreign stocks. Stock ETFs are provided for the sole purpose of providing a diversified opportunity to the investors. While the concept is similar to stock mutual funds, it requires less capital to invest in stock ETFs, as there is a risk involved. On the other hand, stock ETFs will not provide you with ownership of the stocks, and hence, dividends will not be received for your portfolio.

- **Industry ETFs**

  Industry ETFs help investors track specific companies that belong to a particular industry. Industry ETFs will help you understand the uptrends of different sectors by following them. Retail investors invest in technology industry ETFs most of the time because of their exponential growth.

- **Commodity ETFs**

  Futures trading is mainly about investors and businesses worldwide speculating the market price of commodities. You can also buy a set of commodities grouped into an ETF to speculate them as a bunch. Gold, oil, and silver are some commodities that you can group into an ETF. It usually takes much less to hold these ETFs instead of holding them in possession.

- **Currency ETFs**

Currency trading, also known as the Forex market, is the largest financial market globally. In a Forex market, currency pairs such as USD/EUR are traded to regulate the economy. Currency ETFs bunch a few pairs of currencies and let you easily track them. You can group several currencies that are dependent on each other to create a diversified portfolio.

- **Inverse ETFs**

Usually, day traders profit from market price movements by shorting the stock. When you short a stock, you expect a decrease in the stock's price. So, shorting involves borrowing the stock and selling it for a high price to sell it again at a lower price and make profits. Inverse ETFs track huge bets that involve this tactic. Most of the time, the players in inverse ETFs will be banks, corporations, and hedge funds.

- **Index ETFs**

Indexes are financial metrics that track the performance of a group of stocks that are popular with the financial market. For example, S&P 500 is an index that tracks the performance of the top 500 stocks of the U.S. stock market. Index ETFs help you invest in these indexes and earn profits whenever there is an increase in the overall index value.

### *How Do I Invest in ETFs?*

Investing in ETFs is straightforward and can be done from a regular stock exchange or broker. You, however, need to do your research before investing in one of these ETFs.

1. **Find a Platform**

   You can buy or sell ETFs on any investing platform, such as Robinhood. All you have to do is first add a small deposit and then search for the ETFs in the platform. All these exchanges will charge a part of the asset value as a transaction fee. Different brokerages follow different restrictions for other users in their platform to purchase ETFs.

2. **Research ETFs**

   Once your account is eligible to purchase ETFs, you need to start researching them based on differences as mentioned below.

- What is the time frame for you to invest in ETFs?
- What is the primary purpose for you to invest in ETFs? Passive income or long-term growth?
- What are the industries and sectors that you are interested in?

Based on the answers you have given for yourself, create a strategy and search for ETFs with many stocks supporting the factors mentioned.

*Examples:*

There are many popular ETFs for different sectors in the U.S. stock market. If you are trying to invest in ETFs from other countries, you need to verify those locally.

1. **The Invesco QQQ (QQQ)**

   This is an exchange-traded fund that tracks the top 100 technology stocks from the Nasdaq.

2. **The SPDR S&P 500 (SPY)**

   This is a popular and most purchased ETF that tracks the popular S&P 500 index, the most popular 500 publicly traded companies in the U.S. stock market.

# REITs

REITs, or real estate investment trusts, were first created in 1960 by congress to help Americans easily make money with real estate properties to create a steady income. You can benefit from REITs by owning or renting these properties regardless of your financial status. REITs are pretty similar to stock markets, but instead of stocks, the value of a REIT is solely dependent on the rental or home properties. Stockholders help publicly traded companies generate capital, whereas investors involved in REITs help property owners build or maintain these properties for steady income generation.

When you buy REITs, you also do not need to go and visit the properties before buying them. It is now very convenient to virtually research different properties or even look at them using the internet's augmented reality technologies.

REITs are also diverse and provide different ways to invest in them. They can often be divided into equity REITs and mortgage REITs.

1. **Equity REITs**

   When you invest in equity REITs, the most popular REITs, you will often invest in different real estate properties such as offices, shopping malls, and industries. All these properties will generate income from the rent that generates revenue.

2. **Mortgage REITs**

   Mortgage REITs earn revenue by investing in properties that have mortgages. Mortgage REITs can be possible for both commercial and rental properties. When you invest in a mortgage REIT, you will earn high returns if the average interest rate of mortgage value increases. Many investors also invest in mortgage-backed securities to earn some additional income with these REITs.

The security exchange commission should publicly register most REITs before listing their shares for investors to buy in any of the many available stock exchanges. However, some REITs can be made available only for a few private investors even after revisions with the SEC. Every country has its regulations to control how REITs should be traded.

Irrespective of how REITs are distributed, all of them should follow some of the specific rules designed by the SEC. This centralization helps REITs become more popular with investors looking for conservative strategies.

# Chapter 9: Risk Management

Risk is always present when you are investing in a financial asset. Understanding risk and how to overcome risk is essential for maintaining consistent returns as an investor. As the nature of the market itself is unpredictable, there are no proven ways to eliminate risk. However, investors can minimize their risks with practice, experience, and proven strategies.

Every investor should create their own risk management strategy based on their own portfolio. It is impossible to apply risk management principles based on other investors' strategies. Every portfolio needs a specific risk management strategy according to its uncertainty regarding its financial assets.

## What Is Risk Management?

To be precise, risk management is a process to identify the loopholes and uncertainty of your investment decisions and make a shield of strategies to mitigate any future losses. Regardless of the intensity with which they trade, every player in the market should have a risk management strategy to reduce their risk tolerance and not their profits.

Risk is everywhere. There is no asset or financial market without some degree of risk. Risk-free investments such as CDs provide minimal returns to the investors and are not considered good financial practices in the long run.

1. **Plan Your Trades**

   The risk involved with every single trade that you do can be minimized with efficient planning. Planning requires a lot of research and an understanding of the resources available and your position. Planning can also help you hedge your open positions in a much better way. Use tactics such as options trading to help you earn returns even when you lose your portfolio value.

2. **Use Stop Loss and Take Profit**

   Stop-loss and take-profit are automatic price points where your open stock positions can be sold automatically. Stop losses help you to set a lower minimum price to minimize your losses, whereas taking profit will set a maximum price to not decrease your earnings because of further volatility. While both these indicators can help you automate your trades, they can also automatically reduce your returns with extreme changes in the price movement.

3. **2% Trading Rule**

You should never invest all of your capital in just one asset as a trader. Position sizing, also known as the 2% trading rule, is a risk management strategy where an active trade value shouldn't exceed 2% of your total portfolio value. While this strategy can decrease your profits when an asset performs exceptionally well, it gives you more opportunities to test different trades and investments.

4. **Diversify**

Diversification is the most critical trading secret of making profitable returns in the long run. Invest in different assets such as cryptocurrencies, stocks, options, and futures trading to hedge your current open positions. With diversification, you can not only manage risk but also afford risk during uncertain opportunities.

5. **Use Put Options**

While there are different options contracts to hedge your open positions, it is considered a better choice to buy put option contracts for all your valuable assets. Put options contracts will assure you a price value even when the stock performance is not up to your expectations. However, you need to pay a small premium for holding these put option contracts.

## 6. Calculate Returns

Whenever you are making a trade, calculating the expected returns can help you understand both the risk and rewards associated with a financial transaction. Calculating expected returns can also help investors become as rational as possible, and investors will naturally eliminate potential risky trades that provide less and take more if something goes wrong in your predictions when focusing more on returns.

You can use different mathematical formulas related to probability to estimate the returns and additional breakouts if you make a trade. Using support and resistance levels is also recommended if you are an advanced trader with multiple trades.

## 7. Maintain a Trade Journal

Nothing is more critical than retrospection for a trader to minimize risks and increase returns. A trade journal is a perfect way to learn about the principles of sound investments based on your own experiences. No single investor will always win, and hence, there will be many trades that will fall short of your expectations. Note down all these trades and your decisions using an offline or online journal.

A trade journal can also contain technical analysis charts to understand the patterns you may have used to predict the price change.

8. **Add Noncyclic Stocks to Your Portfolio**

Noncyclic stocks don't change their value much irrespective of macroeconomic factors, and they are consistent because they are essential for the world to function efficiently. Including more than 20% of noncyclic stocks in your portfolio can help you to stabilize even during highly volatile market conditions.

9. **Use Pairs Trading**

In a pairs trading strategy, you need to choose two assets in the same sector with high correlation. In pairs trading, an investor usually buys a stock A with a long position and immediately shorts stock B, which is highly correlated with stock A. Only use this strategy when you are sure about the sector's performance but are uncertain about which stocks could perform.

10. **Utilize Algorithmic Trading Bots**

Human knowledge will always be essential for making successful trades. However, it doesn't hurt to use advanced algorithmic technology to automatically find patterns and entry/exit points that can help you minimize the risk in any way possible.

### *How Do I Set Stop-Loss Points More Effectively?*

Many beginners are often confused about the usage of stop-loss points provided by all exchanges to minimize your risk. You can never just casually place a price point for your open positions because of the chance of losing potential profits. Just like making trades as day traders, investors need to place stop-loss points after using technical and fundamental analysis.

*Some of the considerations:*

- Use the moving-average technical indicator to understand the price swing and place a stop-loss based on it.
- Use earning reports and the past market movement for these reports to establish a few stop-loss points for your trades.
- Use a volatility index to estimate the range of stop-loss and take-profit that you can use for a bunch of trades.

## Planning and Importance

For any financial asset, planning is essential. Correct execution of your planning can mitigate losses.

While every investor has their own way of planning their trades, knowing some characteristics can help you prepare better.

- Focus on your goals and choose stocks based on them.
- Research is always essential. Never invest without sufficient research.
- Know about the disadvantages that a particular stock has to offer.
- Always look at the earnings reports and chart patterns associated with historical price changes and movement of the asset.
- All your research should lead to knowing about entry and exit points for your trade.

# Chapter 10: Money Management

Savings make it possible for millions of people to invest at the right time and for a long time. Global catastrophes such as a global pandemic helps people understand why it is essential for people to have savings and an investment portfolio that can help them when they need it. As a beginner investor who is just starting with the investment world, you should focus more on saving money and investing it in the right places. Money management is one of the essential life skills that investors can learn to improve their lifestyle and achieve financial independence at a young age.

## What Are Savings?

The concept of savings is often misunderstood because people usually understand that it is simple and cannot be practiced. However, this is not valid. With enough planning, you can find ways to save money and increase the value over time.

Savings can not only help you to invest effectively but also help you to transform your lifestyle. Money management techniques to grow money and save it for your future investment portfolio should be learned right from your teenage years.

1. **Always Have a Budget**

   It becomes difficult to save money without proper budget planning for your day-to-day tasks. Track all your expenses using mobile apps to understand where you are spending more and need money. Once you get the hang of your total costs, start to budget in a way that at least 20% of the expenses are being cut to help you increase your savings.

2. **Always Follow the Budget**

   Creating a budget is just an initial motivational step to your goal to become financially independent. To follow it, always make wise spending decisions. By an asset only if you think that it is necessary. We are not asking you to make fun of your life, and we want you to be responsible for how much you are spending and how much of it is necessary.

3. **Have a Limit**

   As a teenager, there should always be some limits to understanding how well you are doing with money management. Use these limits to reward yourself whenever you do not cross the boundary. All the unbudgeted spending should be your savings invested in an asset that will guarantee you huge returns in a couple of years.

4. **Always Track Your Spending**

   Once you have budgets and limits and start to follow them, it becomes overwhelming to keep track of all these expenses and effectively understand how well you are saving. To help you be more organized, use either desktop or mobile apps to file everything. You can also use the classic paper and pen method to save all your spending notes in a cabinet. However, we still recommend you go digital to make the process as seamless as possible. Save all your receipts and invoices just by clicking a photo.

5. **Be Safe With Credit Cards**

   Credit cards are necessary and are the most common way of transacting in the real world. However, they can also lure you into spending on items that you don't need. Start to use credit cards only when they are necessary.

6. **Use Coupons While Shopping**

   Another best way to save money in the long run is to keep an eye on the offers and coupons that the businesses provide while you are shopping online. Wait for sales such as the Black Friday sale to get better deals for all your big purchases.

7. **Be Consistent**

   No matter what happens, try to save consistently. Keep a reminder, or you can automate this process in your bank account to automatically invest in SIP. Consistency is the key to increased returns in the future.

8. **Practice**

   Like any other suitable financial practice, saving takes time to get used to. You will figure out ways to save money and invest it in assets that appreciate with time and consistent practice.

## How Do I Grow Money?

To save money, you need to have a source of income. Just having a desk job won't provide you with consistent income. There are many other ways to earn both active and passive income if you are focused on it. As a teenager, you need to know some of these passive income strategies that can help you grow money to invest in financial assets.

1. **Be a Social Media Influencer**

   Social media is everywhere now, and people connect using these platforms. Many teenagers and professionals are earning good money by understanding their target demographics. For example, if you are interested in gaming, you can stream your gameplay using Twitch to earn rewards given by the viewers. Being a social media influencer provides you with a consistent income and can help you earn a brand image that can be further utilized to create business funnels.

2. **Provide Information Through Blogs and Websites**

   People always search for information as they need answers. You can start writing easy-to-understand posts about your favorite topics to earn a dedicated audience for your blogs and websites. Once you have enough audience, you can monetize your content and make money depending on the quality of your information and how consistent you are in providing information.

3. **Learn Marketing**

   No matter which income stream you choose to generate money from, you need to have sufficient knowledge about marketing. Marketing will help you to develop capital unimaginably. Learn about Google Adsense, email marketing, and social media marketing to spread your services to more people.

4. **Create Products and Services**

   This is the most challenging way to grow money, but it will help you create a business that can provide revenue and allow you to create jobs and prosper in the economy. Creating products or services and selling them needs a lot of planning, development, and patience. Have a prototype and get a team of talented individuals to turn prototypes into reality. Many teenagers out there are creating mobile applications and games to generate income.

5. **Partner in a Business**

   If you are not intelligent and thoughtful enough to create your product or business, try to partner with someone who has the skills and energy to make it happen. Help them with capital and ask them for a portion of revenue. Many businesses first came into the limelight because of people willing to help them make their dreams come true. Be that light for people who want it, and you will receive profits when they succeed.

# Conclusion

We are glad that you have decided to achieve financial independence in your teen years. We hope that this book has provided you with enough information to help you make better financial decisions. A few traits need to be learned for an investor to be better than everyone in the market and receive huge returns.

## Important Traits for Investors

1. **Be as Updated as Possible**

   The financial world moves fast, and strategies that work today will not work tomorrow. Read trade magazines and follow famous investors on social media platforms to understand correct market trends. Subscribe to services such as Trends (www.trends.com) to get a premium newsletter for the latest innovative projects among different industries.

2. **Maintain a Strict Schedule**

   It is essential to maintain a strict schedule to reap fruitful results over time as an investor. When you are investing in cryptocurrencies, as the trading time is usually 24 hours round the clock, you need to select a time zone and make your transactions during that time. Using stop losses can also help you to handle challenging situations when you are not around, as these stop losses can automatically close your open positions.

3. **Maintain a Trade Journal**

A trade journal can help you keep track of all your trading decisions over time. Retrospection is very important for investors to make sure that they know about their mistakes and strengths. It is also recommended to relate any research information or charts you have chosen to enter and exit the trade.

4. **Be a Part of the Community**

Investors need to be passionate about the projects they are investing in. For example, if you invested in Polkadot cryptocurrency, then make sure that you join their forums to follow their product development. Following the companies you have invested in on social media platforms can also help you track their products and services. From a business point of view, it is also essential that you research how happy the customers are with their products. Sometimes, earnings reports can be manipulated by higher authorities to sustain their business, so, during these instances, it is vital to check the legitimacy of the earnings by using different strategies.

5. **Learn From Mistakes**

An investor will sometimes face failures. Failures are common in the business world because of the volatility that exists in the market. This is the reason why you shouldn't invest all your money in just one financial asset. Make sure to track your mistakes and find the core reasons for these mistakes. When you see these core reasons, try not to repeat these mistakes in the future.

6. **Maintain a Healthy Lifestyle**

While this may not directly affect your investment decisions, you must have a healthy lifestyle for making investment choices as a career. Eat well, exercise consistently, and take short breaks whenever necessary. Investing in stocks and cryptocurrencies is not a short-term job. It is long-term, and to make a living out of it, you need to know how to balance everything in your life.

7. **Be Patient**

When you invest in a financial asset, you must be patient and give it time for everything to work out as planned. Not all financial assets will have a wild bull run a few days after you invest in it. It takes time and patience to see great results with your investments. However, make sure that the value of your assets is not going down consistently. It is the only red flag you need to be aware of and strictly follow to liquidate your positions.

## 8. Gut vs Research

When investing, many investors feel the dilemma of whether to go with their research or their gut. For beginners, it is highly recommended to go with your research. On the other hand, with experience, you can believe in your gut because your past investment decisions can help you decide whether or not a particular financial decision can work at a definite point. While your gut cannot guarantee your success in the trade, it can help you not regret it when the asset performs well in the future.

## 9. Understand Risks

When you are investing, you should always focus on the risks, irrespective of what financial asset it is. There is no financial asset that can give you huge returns without risk. So, use online risk calculators and find out how much you can lose. Once you are aware of the risks, you can invest in the asset only if you can afford to lose the invested amount.

10. **Be Consistent**

For an investor to become successful and gain financial independence, they need to be consistent. Constantly learn about assets and invest some of your profits in them. With consistency, your overall portfolio value will increase over time.

You are now ready to start your investment journey with any of the assets mentioned in this book. We wish you all the best in your financial journey. Don't forget to do enough research and never stop being hopeful. Always stay hungry and always stay foolish.

**Disclaimer:**

The book's author has written this book only to provide knowledge for the reader. All financial markets are volatile, and hence, readers should not solely depend on this book to make financial decisions. The author of this book will in no way be responsible for the reader's financial decisions.

# References

Dupont, Q. (2019). *Cryptocurrencies and blockchains.* Cambridge Polity.

Hafer, R. W., & Hein, S. E. (2007). *The stock market.* Greenwood Press.

Haslem, J. A. (2010). *Mutual funds: portfolio structures, analysis, management, and stewardship.* Wiley.

Krantz, M. (2016). *Fundamental analysis for dummies.* John Wiley & Sons, Inc.

Markman, J. D. (2001). *Online investing.* Microsoft Press, Cop.

Prypto. (2016). *Bitcoin for dummies.* John Wiley & Sons, Cop.

Schwager, J. D. (1996). *Technical analysis.* Wiley, Cop.

Wild, R. (2016). *Investing in ETFs for dummies.* John Wiley & Sons, Inc.

www.ingramcontent.com/pod-product-compliance
Ingram Content Group UK Ltd.
Pitfield, Milton Keynes, MK11 3LW, UK
UKHW021432280726
14060UKWH00001BA/34